Meluhha

Tree of Life

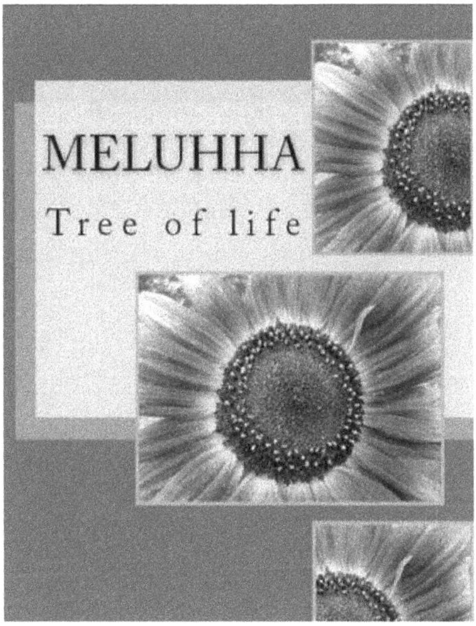

S. Kalyanaraman

Sarasvati Research Center 2013

ISBN 978-0-9911048-0-2

ISBN 10 digits: 0-9911048-0-3

Library of Congress Control Number: 2013920211

Sarasvati Researh Center

Herndon, VA

Meluhha: tree of life

An incomplete inquiry

Hieroglyphs are sacred carvings incised, to convey rebus substantive messages in Meluhha. Symbols associated with divinities and tree of life are Meluhha sacred carvings. Many carvings relate to specific varieties of plants, buds, flowers which are associated with sacredness because they connote -- rebus -- metal artifacts of a *kole.l* 'smithy/forge' which is, *kole.l* 'temple'. Archaeological evidences from Ancient Near East point to the practice of worship in temples of divinities associated with these hieroglyphs. *Kabbalah* of the Ancient Near East is a synonym of *āgama* of Indian tradition with the roots found in Meluhha as a visible language. Both traditions venerate altars as models of temples.

What lessons can be learnt from the evidences to delineate the roots of religious experiences of our ancestors?

This inquiry primarily based on archaeologically attested artifacts is an incomplete religious inquiry.

Kabbalah is a school of thought, a magnificent statement resulting from an intense inquiry into the nature of phenomena including living and non-living forms and cosmic order.

It will clearly be a dialectical exercise to try to compare traditions across communities, extending over millennia of life-experiences.

One thought is apparent and central. There is some energy which permeates the universe and a name ws given to this energy, calling it by various appellations includes divine creation which can only be modeled on hieroglyphs. The hieroglyphs then become attributes of that divinity manifested in the cultural world order.

When a smith forges mineral and metal artifacts, he should have wondered, how come I am able to transmute 'stones'? Competence for diction enables him or her to provide ecstatic, stunning metaphors like Anzu or Inanna. Both Anzu and Inanna could find parallels in living forms but the associated attributes are far too complex to fully comprehend in any one single iconographic detail.

Kabbalah teachings define inner meaning of several attributes identified. The key is 'meaning', the semantics underlying the phenomena which are an extension of the living and non-living phenemona. These phenomena of meanings are an inquiry which find expression in religious observances.

One such observance relates to the metaphor of the altar, a recurrent motif found across cultures and over time.

When the king kneels in adoration in front of an altar which has as the center-piece a mere staff or pole, how did he vocalise the phenomenon which the sculpture has created? Is the sculpture an attempt at representing thought resulting from the inquiry? Or is it just a limited manifestation of the sculptor's life-experience? Or, is it a model of the ziggurat, the temple itself?

Ziggurat as a temple is a leap in inquiry. It is a mere accumulation, a piling up of dhatu, earth forms containing minerals and what is left of minerals, may be ashes, after the processes in the crucible, smithy and forge. Or, is it a memory of accumulated memories bequeathed by ancestors in a life-continuum?

The agama tradition in ancient India also has its roots in inquiry resulting in representation of attributes in human and non-human forms in an architectural model of a temple.

The story of the *agama* and the *kabbalah* has to be fully told to understand the boundaries of the sacred observed and practised as religious experience.

What is the difference between *hakira* (philosophy) and *darash* (inquire, seek, Hebrew: דרש) Is the *darash* traceable to the Indian traditions of *dars'ana*? How do Rabbinic meanings (*midrashic*) explain the traditions evolved over time, narrated in *Tanakh*? Is there a cosmic law?

The sememe darśan has its root dRs', 'to see'. Is the seeing mere visual experience or an experience of the conscious mind? The beholding could be a series of flashes or glimpses seen by the inquirer. The cognate wor *darash* thus becomes a series of events, related or unrelated. events of conscious thought of the devotee.

A fantastic metaphor emerges in the Vis'warupa, divine, wondrous manifestation holding many weapons, ornamented with celestial flowers and perfumes. Before such a form, the devotee kneels down in adoration, like Tukulti-Ninurta I (1243-1207

BCE), King of Assyria or like Arjuna in front of Sri Krishna as narrated in the Mahabharata and the Gita.

In Sumerian tradition, an earlier inquiry related to Ninurta (Nin Ur, divinity of war). He is also rendered as Ninib or Ninip and identified with the sun divinity or as Nimrod. In Nippur, there is indication that Ninurta was part of a triad of Enlil and Ninlil (harvest divinity). When Ninurta is depicted on friezes, he is shown holding a bow and arrow, a sickle or sword or a mace named Sharur. Sharuru can assume the form of a winged lion, later called Shedu. In the agama tradition, divinities hold many weapons and tools produced in the smithy-forge. When the artisan builds a kolel 'temple', he or she presents divine attributes as metaphors of the divine holding many artifacts coming out of the crucible and the anvil, thanks to the interventio of the artificer who was originally a mere stone-worker. He or she now holds a sacred pot containing the alchemical stone capable of achieving transmutation from being to becoming.

See Ninurta's exploits, a transliterated text of *Ninurta's exploits: a šir-sud (?) to Ninurta.*[1]

"Ninurta slays each of the monsters later known as the "Slain Heroes" (the Warrior Dragon, the Palm Tree King, Lord Saman-ana, the Bison-beast, the Mermaid, the Seven-headed Snake, the Six-headed Wild Ram), and despoils them of valuable items such as Gypsum, Strong Copper, and the Magilum boat). Eventually, Anzû is killed by Ninurta who delivers the Tablet of Destiny to his father, Enlil."[2]

magilum [BOAT] (5x: Old Babylonian) wr. ^{ĝeš}ma$_2$-gi$_4$-lum; ^{ĝeš}ma$_2$-gi-lum; ^{ĝeš}ma$_2$-gi-la$_2$ "a boat" Akk. *magillu*

[1]  ^{ĝeš}ma$_2$-gi$_4$-lu

[2]  ^{ĝeš}ma$_2$-gi-lum

[3] 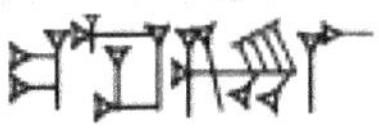 ^{ĝeš}ma$_2$-gi-la$_2$

~ ELA/Ur III/Umma **ma$_2$-lah$_5$ ma$_2$-gi-lum-ma-še$_3$** AUCT 3, 501 2.

Akk. *magillu* "type of boat, barge".[3]

Ninurta's return to Nibru: a šir-gida to Ninurta[4] provides the narrative: "55-63. He (Lord Ninurta) hung the Six-headed wild ram on the dust-guard. He hung the Warrior dragon on the seat. He hung the Magilum boat on the .... He hung the Bison on the beam. He hung the Mermaid on the foot-board. He hung the Gypsum on the forward part of the yoke. He hung the Strong copper on the inside pole pin (?). He hung the Anzud bird on the front guard. He hung the Seven-headed serpent on the shining cross-beam. 64-69. Lord Ninurta stepped into his battle-worthy chariot..."

Is there any significance or meaning assignable, from this narrative, which refers to artifacts of gypsum, strong copper and the Magilum boat of Meluhha fame, apart from Anzu who had stolen the tablet of destiny? It appears that Meluhhan artificer who created a writing system referred to strong copper by using the rebus metaphor of the sunflower, *karaDa* which also connoted 'strong copper' or hard alloy. When copper was hardened by alloying, it became 'useful' or 'meaningful' as a resource for making weapons and tools or as a resource for engaging in trade transactions using the Magilum boat.

Was the six-headed wild ram the pictorial rendering of a set of six antelopes presented in a circle on a Persian Gulf seal or on Indus writing tablet?

This is no ordinary boat. It is Sumerian ship of the netherworld. Ninurta seized this boat and hung it on his chariot. The pictorial representation of the narrative has not been unearthed so far.

From being to becoming is the central theme of both kabbalah and dars'ana traditions. It is a historical challenge indeed to unravel the nature of interactions among communities which evolved these 'received' traditions.

The exercise in hermeneutics has just begun. This is an incomplete inquiry. The inquiry can progress as we unravel the vocalised expressions about this inquiry by our ancestors, revealed, for example on hieroglyphs of Ancient Near East and Indo-Eurasian writing systems.

Like the journey on the Magilum boats, this inquiry into the nature of human thought, darash or dars'ana, has to start from the evidence bequeathed to us by our ancestors.

Tree of life is associated with Inana. A cylinder seal inscribes Inanna's Descent

Mesopotamian cylinder seal. Hematite.2000-1600 BCE.

Meluhha hieroglyphs on this cylinder seal are:

Centerpiece: Inanna: pudendum muliebre, horns on

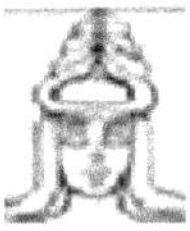

the crown

kola 'woman' Rebus: *kol* 'working in iron'

kuṭhi 'pudendum muliebre, vagina' Rebus: *kuṭhi* 'smelting furnace'.

kirīṭa ' diadem, crest ' Rebus: *kirāṭa* m. ' merchant ' (also, name of a people *kirāta* who spoke a *Prākrit*, may be *Meluhha/Mleccha*) *koḍ* 'horn' (Santali); rebus: *koḍ* 'workshop'

Ligatured hieroglyphs and associated symbols read rebus as catalog of a smithy's repertoire:

aryeh 'lion' kōl stick, staff, branch, arrow . *eraka* 'wing'; ढालकाठी [ḍhālakāṭhī] ढालखांब *m* A flagstaff; esp.the pole for a grand flag or standard. Rebus: *āra* 'brass'; *eraka* 'copper'; *ḍhāla* ' shield ' ḍhālako 'large ingot'.

mlekh 'goat' Rebus: milakkha 'copper'. *ḍāṛhū* m., *dāṛū*, 'pomegranate' Rebus:

ḍhāḷako 'large ingot'.

Human face ligatured to fish. Turtle on top. *mũh* 'face' Rebus: *mũh* 'ingot'; ayo 'fish' Rebus: ayo 'metal, iron'; turtle or tortoise *kamaṭhamu* 'A tortoise'.

Rebus: *kammaṭa* (Kannada)

కమటము *kamaṭamu*. [Telugu] 'A portable furnace for melting the precious metals.' అగసాలెవాని కుంపటి. (Telugu) *kampaṭṭa* 'mint'.

mũh 'face' Rebus: *mũh* 'ingot'; ayo 'fish' Rebus: ayo 'metal, iron'; ram मेंढा [mēṇḍhā] *m* (मेष S through H) A male sheep, a ram or tup.(Marathi) *meḍ* 'iron' (Mundari. Remo.) Thus, the cylinder seal assigns divine attributes to the forge and the crucible. Profane symbols become divine, sacred hieroglyphs. Hierophany means 'revelation of the sacred'. Manifestation of the sacred is not mere commemoration on rebus inscriptions but participation in the performance of worship. Such performance of worship is evidenced in the scores of temples for divinities with the ziggurat as the pinnacle of representation of worship of ancestors, standing testament of the evolution of sacred religious life related to profane living of hard work sith *dhātu* 'minerals. Hence, the designation of a *stūpa* as *dhātugarbha 'womb of minerals'* – a metaphor which finds expression on Meluhha writing and inscriptions. Ziggurats are also expressions of wonder at the phenomena of nature which allow for transmutation of minerals into metals and forging of metallic weapons and tools for transforming patterns of living.

Vase decorated with nude goddesses, known as the "Ishtar vase".[5]

karaṇḍa 'duck' (Sanskrit) *karaṛa* 'a very large aquatic bird' (Sindhi) Rebus: करडा [karaḍā] Hard from alloy--iron, silver &c. (Marathi)

Stele representing the goddess Ishtar of Irbil

Sumerian goddess Inanna, who was known as Ishtar among the Akkadians. Many mythological poems were dedicated to her, making her the preeminent goddess. Combining the symbolism of fertility and the

power of the warrior-woman, she was venerated by the kings of both Assyria and Babylon, and throughout Mesopotamia's long history this religious fervor never waned.

A stupa is a temple. So is the stupa mound found at Mohenjodaro. It is possible that this stupa was in place during the mature phase of the civilization, comparable to the Ur ziggurat.

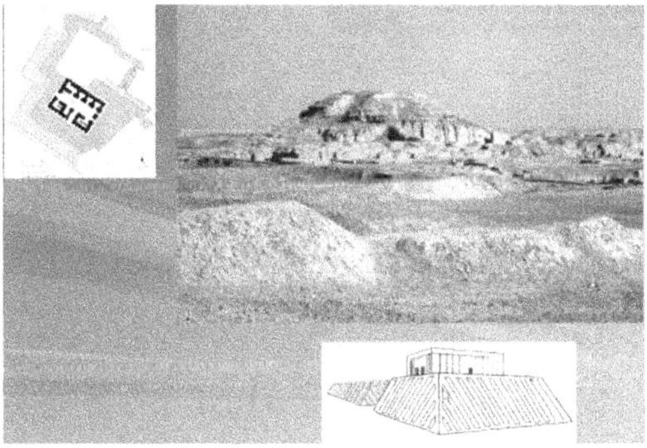

Ziggurat, Uruk.[6]

An extraordinary event has been reported which links the evidences from the past to present-day botanical experiment.

Bringing a piece of ancient history of tree of life, back to life

A report on an ongoing, astonishing experiment to find out that date seeds can stay alive for nearly two millennia provides the backdrop for an excursus on the 'tree of life' or 'sacred tree' – a leitmotif which has moulded civilizations for millennia. This is a tribute to Dr. Elaine Solowey and Dr. Sarah Solowey for bringing a piece of ancient civilization back to life.

Credit: Chronicle Graphic. Photos Credit: by David Blumenfeld, Special to The Chronicle. A news report datelined June 12, 2005 had chronicled how the seed of an extinct date palm sprouted after 2000 years into a 14 inches high plant. The photos show the germinated date tree and Dr. Elaine Solowey and Dr. Sarah Solowey holding the date tree grown from the seed obtained from Masada, an ancient Jewish

Archaeological site.[7]

An amazing report appeared on February

14, 2013 and again on October 7, 2013 about an ancient date palm tree which flourishes again.[8] At the site of Herod the Great's mountaintop palace at Masada near the Dead Sea in Israel, the late Ehud Netzer discovered in 1973 a clay jar which contained a cache of seeds which had been stored ca. 2000 years ago. Working in collaboration with Louis L. Borick Natural Medicine Center at Hadassah Hospital in Jerusalem, Elaine Solowey who is a botanical researcher received one of the seeds for experimental planting. Solowey planted it in a pot at Kibbutz Ketura on the Jewish festival of trees which fell on Jan. 25, 2005. The seedling sprouted about four weeks after planting. It produced the first blossom in 2011 and is now a young date tree shown in the photograph. The tree has been nick-named 'Methuselah' as a tribute to the oldest person of the Biblical account. Ancient Hebrews called the palm a 'tree of life'. Romans called it Phoenix dactylifera, 'the date-bearing phoenix' referring to its survival for eternity even in desert lands while other plants died.[9]

Plant as a hieroglyph is evidenced in many archaeological artifacts of Ancient Near East. Mircea Eliade who was a professor at the University of Chicago propounded a theory of hierophacies to explain the bases of religion, contrasting human experience of reality in sacred and profane spaces and time.[10]

Pomegranate, bunch of twigs as hieroglyphs

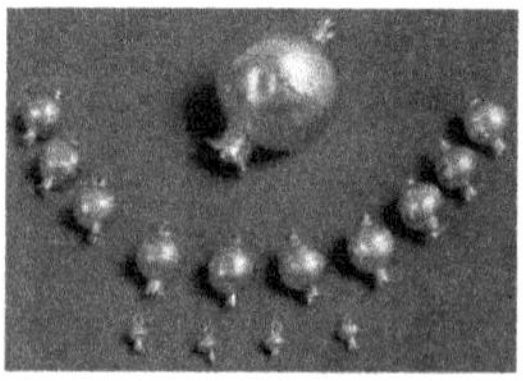

Cast gold pomegranates from Tomb 1.[11] Gold ornaments in the shape of pomegranate (*nurmu*, QI 208), Nimrud, Tomb I; 8th c.; diam. of largest ornament 4.5 cm. gross wt. or remaining fourteen ornaments 26.59 g; largest ornament IM 109011, remaining ornaments IM 108973.[12]

Pomegranate. Metropolitan Museum. Period:Neo-Assyrian Date:ca. 9th–8th century BCE. Geography: Mesopotamia, Nimrud (ancient Kalhu) Culture: Assyrian Medium: Ivory Dimensions:1.3 in. (3.3 cm) Classification:Ivory/Bone-SculptureCredit Line:Rogers Fund, 1954 Accession Number:54.117.7[13]

A Neo-Assyrian relief, a detail of a throne and the

hand of the carrying attendant, from Dur Sharrukin (Khorsabad), 721-705 B.C.

S. *ḍāṛhū* m., P. *dāṛū*, 'pomegranate' Rebus: *ḍhāḷako* 'large ingot' (Gujarati)

Nimrud dominated Mesopotamia from 10th century BCE down to 612 BCE. Also found was a glittering gold tiara with the 'rosette' motifs. The tiara was found in the tomb of Queen Yaba, the wife of Tiglath-Pileser III, who ruled from 744 to 727 BCE.

After Fig. 2.22, Gansell 2008; Ivory relief portraying a

winged woman wearing a robe; Arslan Tash; 8th c.; h. 7.8 cm, w. 5.5 cm; Karlsruhe 72/40[14]
She holds a bunch of twigs in her right hand.

eṟake, eṟaṅke, ṟakke, ṟekke wing (Kannada). Rebus: *eraka* 'copper'. *kūṭī* = bunch of twigs (Skt.) *kuṭhi* 'smelting furnace' (Santali)

Ancient Near Eastern oikumene and the sacred tree

Oikumene, is derived from a Greek verb meaning "to inhabit," and refers to the inhabited part of the world.

Simo Parpola begins his inquiry into the meaning of the Assyrian tree of life using symbolism of numbers and orthographic features as the styles evolved from fourth millennium BCE: "A stylized tree with obvious religious significance already occurs as an art motif in fourth-millennium Mesopotamia, and, by the second millennium BCE, it is found everywhere within the orbit of the ancient Near Eastern oikumene, including Egypt, Greeceand the Indus civilization. The meaning of the motif is not clear, but its overall composition strikingly recalls the Tree of Life of later Christian, Jewish, Muslim, and Buddhist art. The questio of whether the concept of the Tree of Life actually existed in ancient Mesopotamia has been debated, however, and thus many scholars today prefer the more neutral term 'sacred tree' when referrig to the Mesopotamian tree."[15] Simo Parpola goes on to explain the Sefirotic Tree of Life in Kabbalah – a doctrinal structure which evolved ca. 1st century CE, by noting that Sefirot literally means 'countings' or 'numbers' which are a count of divine powers or 'attributes' manifested in the King. One interpretation is that the tree itself is a representation of divine world order, an image of God. Another is that the tree also represents the ideal man in the image of God. Scholars have debated if the symbolism of the tree in Kabbalah was a borrowing from a Mesopotamian model. Simo Parpola presents a reconstructed tree, paralleling the Kabbalah tree of attributes with the Mesopotamian divinities and their corresponding attributes. The attributes are often found associated in assyriological studies.

Tree as Sunflower. 72 names of God are inscribed on its petals. From Athanasius Kitcher, Oedipus Aegypticus, Rome, 1652; Ponee, Kabbalah, p.177.(After Fig. 6a Simo Parpola, 1993, p. 175).

Jack M. Sasson held a panel discussion on Simo Parpola's theory. A report on this discussion appears in a paper by Jerrold S. Cooper.[16] Cooper notes the absence of textual referenes to Mesopotamian iconographic items. Gruenwald notes that despite Simo Parpola's arguments, 'the meaning and the sense of 'structure' – that is, the inner grammar – is still missing, unless someone provides the necessary informative details.' Gruenwald concludes that the emergence of the Kabbalah at the end of the twelfth century is still a mystery.

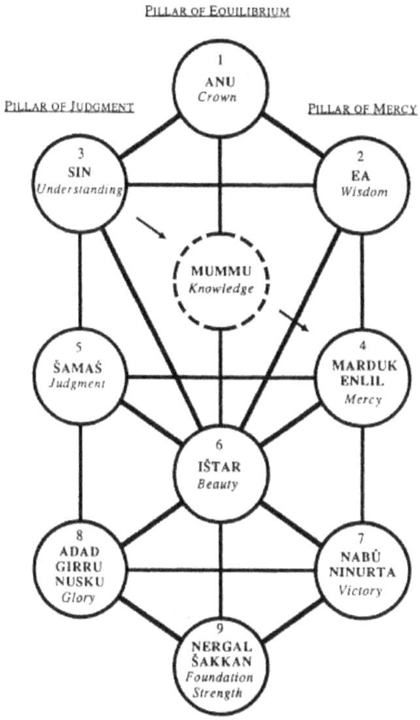

H. York makes a general survey of iconography of the ancient East and finds a long tradition which extended far and wide in Indo-Eurasia.[17] Christine Kepiski presents Egyptian evidence which dates from the sixteenth century BCE and Greek examples which are also comparable to the Babylonian forms.[18] These studies, however, do not deal with the meaning of the 'tree' motif.

Tree of life carving. Hazor. 8th century BCE bone handle carving depicting the tree of life, a date palm.[19] Bronze standard showing snakes. Bronze standard from Hazor showing the head of a goddess and two snakes.[20]
arā 'snake' Rebus: *āra* 'brass'.

Structural elements of the Assyrian Tree Motif (After Fig. 1, Simo Parpola, 1993, p.162)

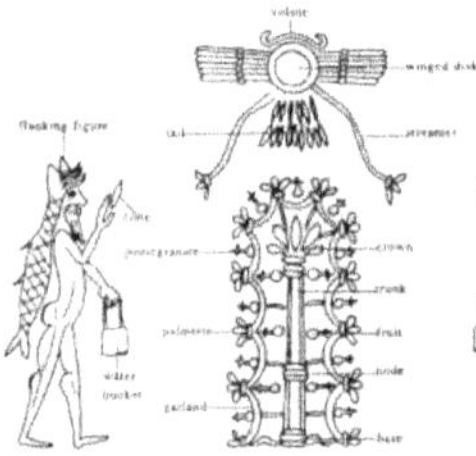

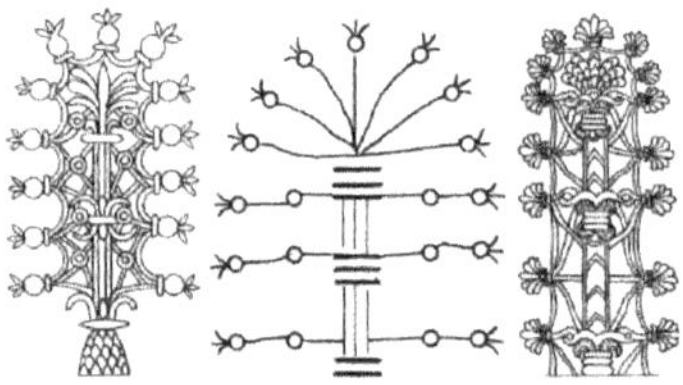

Triadic configuration of Nodes, Volutes, and Circles (After Fig. 2, Simo Parpola, 1993, p. 162).

Model of a temple of Astarte, a deity worshipped by Phoenicians

Winged lions are shown on tiers 1 and 3 on one side of the stand. Drawing by Stephanie Beaulieu after Gadon 1989: 174, #97. 10th cent. BCE. Incense holder from Taanach, with symbols of Inanna and Hathor surmounted by a radiant calf. Terracotta Asherah 11th – 6th cent. BCE (Gaddon, Pritchard 1954). Taanach cult stand: This 3-foot-high, terra-cotta stand, from the late-tenth-century B.C.E. Israelite site of Taanach, has four tiers. The second

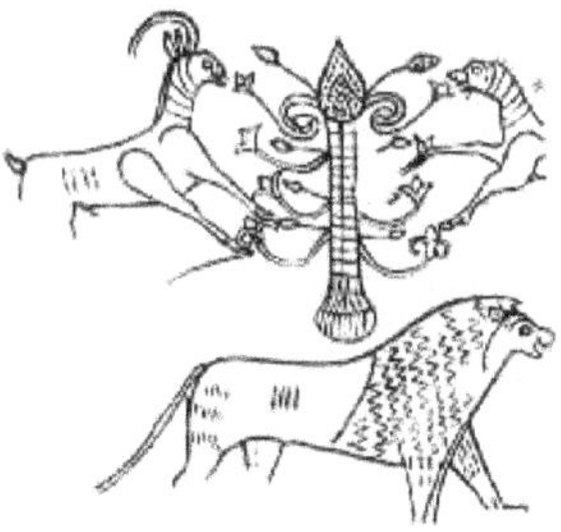

tier from the bottom shows two sphinxes, which may represent the cherubim that adorned the Jerusalem Temple (see 1 Kings 8:6–7). The bottom tier has two lions flanking a female figure—

possibly the Canaanite goddess Asherah, who is often described as riding on the back of a lion. Pedestal for the figure of a deity Taanach Iron Age I, 10th century BCE Pottery H: 53.7; W: 22; L: 24.5 cm Staff Archaeological Officer in the Civil Administration of Judea and Samaria Accession number: K4197[21]

From the Taanach Stand - Tier 2 (a cult stand from Taanach in Northern Ancient Israel), two ibexes eating from the Tree of Life - a possible Asherah motif (compare the "wooden" Asherah items forbidden in the Bible): Tree of life flanked by two ibex on tier 2. A sacred tree remarkably similar to that on tier 2 also appears on Pithos A from Kuntillet 'Ajrud.

Fierce lions appear on the edges of the Taanach scenes, while a maned lion strides below the tree on the *pithos* drawing.[22]

This two-foot-high, square, hollow cult stand from late 10th-century B.C.E. Taanach contains two depictions of the goddess Asherah. The first is a nude woman in the middle of the left bottom register. She appears again in the third register from the bottom, this time as a branching tree flanked by ibexes. Both this and the bottom register feature lions on the outside column, an association seen in other depictions of Asherah. Author Ruth Hestrin traces the development of this important goddess's iconography in *Understanding Asherah.*[23]

A surmise is that the composition may depict the goddess known as Asherah, Yahweh's consort: the nude woman on tier 4. If the animal is a bull calf, it could be a symbol of Baal or Yahweh. On its back is a sun disk—embellished with either wings or rays. The composition is flanked by two posts with curved tops comparable to the reeds shown on Warka vase.

The vacant space in the center of tier 3 of the Taanach stand is protected by cherubim.[24]

A terracotta censer, found at Tell Taanach / Ta'anek, Israel. 13th-12th century BCE. A ritual object, possibly

Canaanite; found broken with sling stones which is interpreted as indicating a change in religious beliefs. Istanbul Archaeological Museum, Turkey. The tree symbol flanked by two goats on either side, compares with the symbol shown on tier 2 of the stand which is a model of a temple for Astarte.

Veneration of sacred tree in Ancient Near East

Neo-Assyrian alabastrine limestone relief from Room I

of the North-West Palace of Assurnasirpal II (883-859 BCE), Nimrud (ancient Khalhu). H.77.5 cm. Vatican Museums, inv. 14989 *Kneeling winged genius worshipping the tree of life*

The reign of Assurnasirpal II marks the first great flourishing of Neo-Assyrian figurative art, which is expounded in the decoration of the monumental Royal Palace that the sovereign had erected at the north-western extremity of the Acropolis of Nimrud, the ancient Kalhu. The two reliefs exhibited belong to the slabs dedicated to the mythical-symbolic theme of the adoration of the Sacred Tree, a symbol of the regality which is the bearer of fecundity and life.[25]

Kabbalah (Hebrew: קַבָּלָה, literally "receiving/tradition" has an almost equivalent synonym in Meluhha. It is *āgama*.

One example of the tradition is hanukkha (menorah) (Hebrew: מנורת חנוכה *m'noraht khanukkah*, pl. *menorot*) (also Hebrew: חֲנֻכִּיָּה *hanukiah*,

or *chanukkiyah*, pl. *hanukiyot*/ *chanukkiyot*. The ninth holder, called the *shamash* ("helper" or "servant"), is for a lamp used to light all other. Shamash is Akkadian sun divinity. A synonym in Sumerian is *utu*.

A Philistine altar discovered in 2011at the Tell Tzafit archaeological site. 1 meter high and ½ meter long. The stone altar is from the 9th century BCE and identified with the biblical Philistine city of Gat. The discovery was made by Prof Aren Maeir of the Land of Israel and Archaeology studies at Bar-Ilan University.[26]

In the Indian tradition, the sun hieroglyph was shown

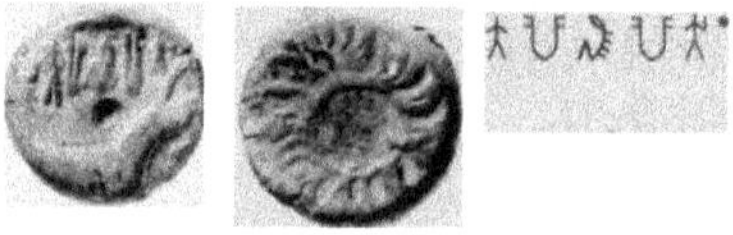

on a two-sided Mohenjo-daro tablet M0428b.

m0428At m0428Bt 1607. Sun is the radiating solar symbol. In the context of metallurgy and trade, the hieroglyph connoted: arka, 'sun'; 'flash, sun' (Rigveda; root arch ,'pray'); akka 'sun' (Pali. Prakrit); āk 'sun' (Maithili); aṟkaṉ 'sun' (Tamil); aka 'lightning' (Sinhala); inscription: vid-aki 'lightning flash' (Sinhala) Rebus: arka, akka 'copper', 'metal' (Kannada); arukkam 'copper' (Tamil) akka 'metal' (Telugu) arka 'copper' (Sanskrit) akkaśālai 'metal works, mint' (Tamil); akkaśālaiyar 'goldsmiths, jewellers' (Tamil) akaśāle 'business, workshop of gold- or silver-smith' (Kannada) eraka 'copper'.

Shamash in his shrine, his emblem before him on the altar

The Tablet of Shamash is a stone tablet recovered from the ancient Babylonian city of Sippar in southern Iraq in 1881; it is now a major piece in the British Museum's ancient Middle East collection. It is dated to the reign of King Nabu-apla-iddina ca. 888 – 855 BCE.

The tablet is 29.21 centimetres (11.50 in) long by

17.78 centimetres (7.00 in) wide and was recovered during the excavations by Hormuzd Rassam between 1878 to 1883. The tablet was found complete, but already broken into two large and six small pieces by the time of King Nabopolassar, between 625 and 605 BC. He replaced it with a new one and placed the original in an inscribed earthenware casket along with some related items and interred then under the asphalt temple floor.[2] It was encased in a clay cast or "squeeze" that created impressions when placed over the face of the stone and protected it. This indicates that the tablet was an item of reverence, possibly stored due to newer traditions. The tablet has serrated edges like a saw, which was the symbol of both Shamash and Saint Simon Zelotes in later tradition.[27]

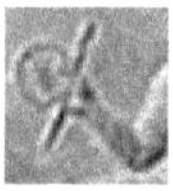

The symbols of measuring rod and cord associated with Shamash (Utu, Sumerian) are significant and may relate to *kaḍiyo, kaḍiyaṇa* Meluhha glosses which refer to a mason, bricklayer, an architect/designer/builder. Sun is visualized by the artist as an architect of the cosmos.

Northern gate. Sanchi Stupa shows

two glyphs. One is the architect carrying a rod (mace?) and cod. The other is the hieroglyphic representation of the temple. On the edge is a seated lion. The bas-relief on the top of the obverse (pictured) shows Shamash, the Sun God, beneath symbols of the Sun, Moon and Venus. He is depicted in a seated position in a shrine, holding forward a measuring rod and reel of cord. There is another large sun disk in front of him on an altar, suspended from above by two figures. Of the three other figures on the left, the central one is dressed in the same fashion as Shamash and is assumed to be the Babylonian king Nabu-apla-iddina receiving the symbols of deity. The cuneiform text beneath the stele is divided into fifteen passages, blending prose, poetic and rhetorical elements in the fashion typical of Mesopotamian royal inscriptions. It tells how Sippar and the Ebabbar temple of Shamash had fallen into disrepair with the loss of the statue of the God. This cult image is temporarily replaced with the solar disk; it is further described how a new figure of Shamash was found in an eastern part of the Euphrates, from which Nabu-apla-iddina has constructed a new statue of lapis lazuli and gold to restore the cult.

Similar iconographic and prosaic parallels have been evidenced from Mesopotamian and later Jewish sources where the king who restores the cult is seen like a deity passing on divine symbols. The remainder of the text records the gifts of the royal grant, similar to a *kudurru* and discusses the practices of the temple, priestly rules, dress codes and regulations.[28] Drawn by Faucher-Gudin, from a photograph by Rassam. The busts of the two deities on the front of the roof of the shrine are the two charioteers of the sun; they uphold and guide the rayed disk upon the altar. Cf. in the Assyrian period the winged disks led with cords by two genii.[29]

Assyrian tree of life bears pomegranates

Relief panel Period: Neo-Assyrian. Ca. 883-859 BCE. Mesopotamia, Nimrud (Ancient Kalhu). Gypsum alabaster. Holds a punch of symbols of ligatured pomegranate and safflower.

This is an example of a seal ringed with pomegranats as published by D. Diringer, `*Le Inscrizioni antico-ebraiche palestinesi* in 1934, Tav. 19:24, Florence: Felice le Monnier. [BASOR, 220, 1975, p. 65] [30]

In his

excavation at Sherif Khan, Assyrian Tarbasu, Layard discovered this well-preserved cylinder seal whose 3 line inscription names its owner as "Muses-Ninurta" (or as read by Tallqvist and others, `Musezib-Ninurta'), son of Ninurta-eres, grandson of Samanuha-sar-ilani, and designates all three as "priest-princes". In a well planned rendition, a pomegranate tree stands in the center beneath the man in the winged sun, and on each side a king in a pose of adoration; each holds a band emanating from the sun and ending in an omega-shaped hand. Behind the king stands an eagle-man with an eagle-head and wings, protecting the ruler. While this cylinder seal is not expressly identified by Layard himself as being from the finds at Tarasu (*Ninive und Babylon*, p. 603), Hommel (*Geschichte*, 1885, pp. 557-8) does make that identification. [Seal of chalcedony, H. 5.08 cm, diameter 2.54 cm, Mansell, Phot. 595, Br. Mus. No. 89135. See further Unger in Ebert, RLV XI, 181.; in Eckhard Unger's, *Two Seals of the 9th Century BC From Shadikanni on the Habur* in BASOR, No. 130, April 1953, p. 16.] [31] The frieze shows pomegranate motif on the sword held by the left hand, close the waist-belt. "Relief from the N.W. palace of Ashurnasirpal II (883-859 BCE) showing anointing of the Tree of Life. A winged god holds what appears to be a pinecone and a pot with the anointing oil. Above the Tree of Life is the royal signet of the god Ashur. The god Ashur is depicted as a man with a bow inside a winged solar disk or as a winged solar disk."[32] The accompanying inscription refers to 'vice-regent -- *iṣṣakku* -- of Aṣṣur', perhaps a reference to the divine sanction to the ruler signified by the winged disk hovering above the sacred tree.

Simo Parpola notes that in some depictions, the Tree symbolized the divine world order and the king was portrayed as the human personification of the tree.[33]

Stone relief from the throne room of Ashurnasirpal II [quote]Nimrud (ancient Kalhu), northern Iraq Neo-Assyrian, 870–860 BC This Assyrian relief comes from the throne room of the so-called North-West Palace of Ashurnasirpal II (reigned 883-859 BC) at Nimrud in northern Iraq. It was originally positioned behind the king's throne. Ashurnasirpal himself appears twice, shown from two sides, dressed in ritual robes and holding a mace symbolising his authority. The figure of the king on the right makes a gesture of worship to a god in a winged disk in the top centre of the relief. The god, who is the source of the king's power, may be Ashur, the national god, or Shamash, the god of the sun and justice. He holds a ring in one hand, an ancient Mesopotamian symbol of god-given kingship. The figure of the king on the left appears to gesture towards a so-called Sacred Tree which dominates the centre of the relief. This balanced combination of steams and foliage is a symbol of fertility and abundance given by the gods. Behind the king, on either side of the relief, is a winged protective spirit who blesses and purifies Ashurnasirpal using a cone-shaped object to sprinkle liquid from a ritual bucket. The relief thus summarises visually the main ideas of Assyrian kingship; he is the source of abundance provided by the gods. Ancient visitors approaching the enthroned king would have thus seen three royal figures, the living king facing them, and, either side of him, two carved images showing Ashurnasirpal's relationship with the gods. Emerging from behind the king himself would be the Sacred-Tree. There was another almost identical relief opposite the main door of the throne room, and similar scenes occupied prominent positions in other Assyrian palaces. They were also embroidered on the royal clothes.[34] [unquote]

It is possible that the capsules on the head-dress of a Minoan goddess, connote pomegranates as argued by William A. Emboden, Jr.[35] The tree of life bears pomegranates.

Plaque: winged creatures, stylized trees. Metmuseum. ca. 8th–7th century B.C.E. Gold. H. 21.2 cm.[36]

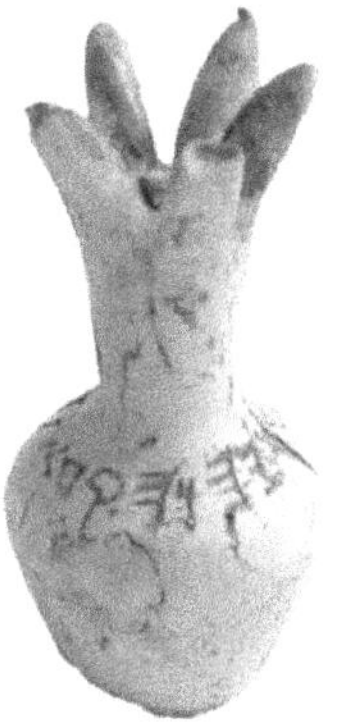

Carved piece of ivory in the shape of a

pomegranate. Could have been used as a scepter top piece evidenced by the hole in its base. Israel Museum, Jerusalem. Said to belong to the temple of Yahweh. Dated according to its textual style to 8th century BCE. (Genuineness, controversial).[37]

Cylinder seal with the solar disk of Ashur, anointing with two eagle-headed gods before the Tree of Life. The blossoms on the tree appear to be pomegranates. The Divine stream is shown emanating from the winged disk above the stylized tree. The streams end with the symbol of 'thunderbolt weapon' close to the fifth row of pomegranates emanating from the tree. The bucket is *banduddu*; the cone is *mullilu* and are used for purification. The unresolved debate relates to the identification of the 'cone' -- as a date flower or as a pine cone -- held by the divinities in their spouted right hands.

Simo Parpola presents many glyptic variants of the

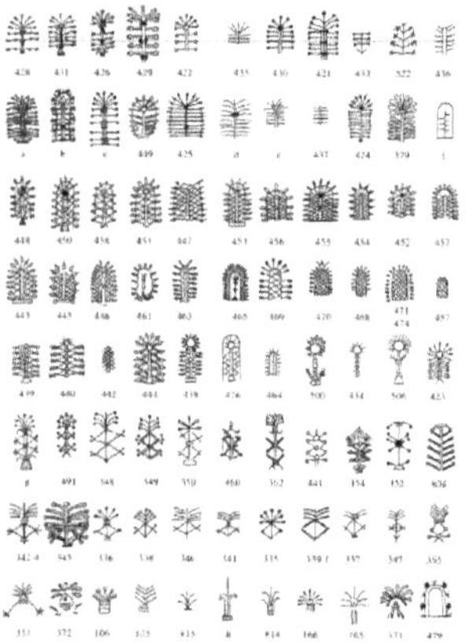

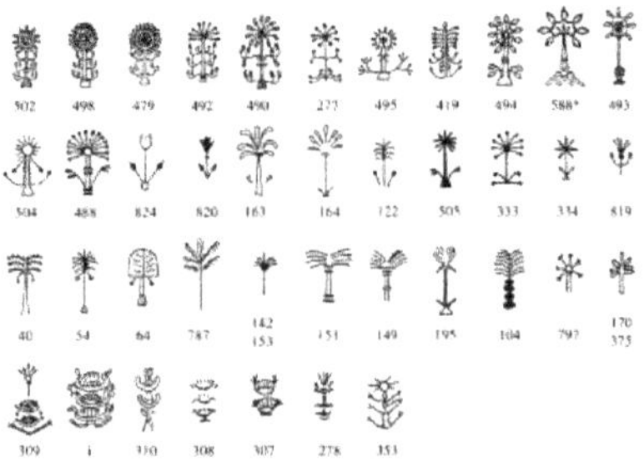

Assyrian Tree.

(After Fig. in Appendix A, Simo Parpola, 1993, pp. 200-201).

Tree, plants, flowers, fruits as rebus hieroglyphs in bronze-age writing traditions

A flower with five petals is stylized on this potsherd which constitutes an writing system dated to ca. 3500 BCE and thus could pre-date all known writing systems such as Proto-Elamite or Cuneiform. This is a hieroglyph read rebus: tagara 'tabernae Montana, fragrant wild tulip' Rebus: tagara 'tin' (an alloying mineral which alloys with copper to create tin-bronze which replaced the scarce arsenical bronze.)

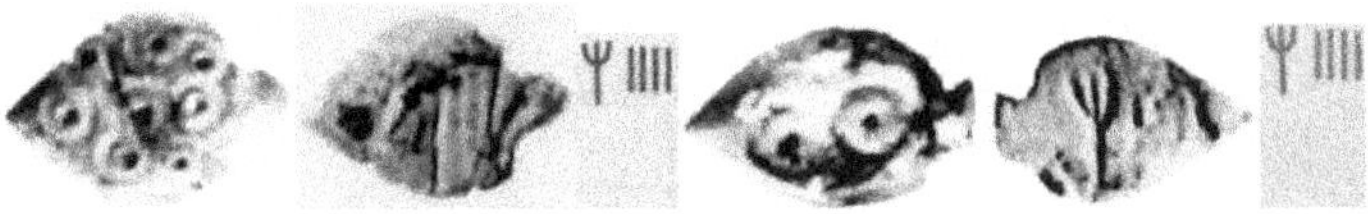

h337, h338 Texts 4417, 4426 (les on leaf-shaped tablets)

Text 8031Kalibangan seal K050. scarf (on pigtail); body of a tiger, a human body with bangles on arm, a pig-tail, horns of a markhor crowned by a twig. *dhaṭu* ,*dhaṭhu*) 'scarf' (WPah.) Rebus: *dhātu* 'mineral' (Sanskrit), *dhatu* id. (Santali). Headgear: markhor horns crowned by a twig. *miṇḍhāl* 'markhor' (Torwali) Rebus: *mẽṛhẽt, meḍ* 'iron' *ispat mẽṛhẽt* 'steel' (Munda. Santali) *kūṭī* = bunch of twigs (Sanskrit) *kuṭhi* 'smelting furnace' (Santali) *kola* 'tiger' Rebus: *kol* 'working in iron';'alloy of five metals'. *kola* 'woman' Rebus: *kol* 'working in iron'. Thus, the glyphic composition is a catalog of a smithy working with metal alloys.

The association of the gloss kola with meanings 'woman, tiger' is remarkably demonstrated on a ligatured sculpture.

Feline figurine. Terracotta. A woman's face and headdress are shown. The base has a hole to display it on a stick. (After Kenoyer, JM; courtesy: Dept. of Archaeology and museums, Govt. of Pakistan). *kola* 'woman, tiger' *kōlupuli* 'Bengal tiger' Rebus: *kol* 'working in iron'; 'five metal alloy, *pañcaloha*).

Mohenjo-daro Seals m1186, m0304. A bunch of twigs

constitute the headger of the person seated in penance, with a scarf. One is seated on a bovine-hoofed platform.

kamaḍhaga, kamaḍhaya = a type of penance (Prakrit) Rebus: kamaṭamu, kammaṭamu = a portable furnace for melting precious metals; kammaṭīḍu = a goldsmith, a silversmith (Telugu) kãpṛauṭ jeweller's crucible made of rags and clay (Bi.); kampaṭṭam coinage, coin, mint (Tamil) kamaṭhāyo = a learned carpenter or mason, working on scientific principles; *kamaṭhāṇa* [cf. karma, kām, business + *sthāna, thāṇam*, a place

fr. Sanskrit *sthā* to stand] arrangement of one's business; putting into order or managing one's business (Gujarati) A soft-stone flask, 6 cm. tall, from Bactria (northern Afghanistan) showing a winged female deity (?) flanked by

two flowers similar to those shown on the comb from Tell Abraq.[38]

Wild tulip motif. A motif that occurs on southeast Iranian cylinder seals and on Persian Gulf seals. 1st row: Bactrian artifacts; 2nd row: a comb from the Gulf area and late trans-Elamite seals.[39] Bone comb with Mountain Tulip motif and dotted circles. TA 1649 Tell Abraq, United Arab Emirates. Ivory comb with Mountain Tulip motif and dotted circles. TA 1649 Tell Abraq.[40] The ivory comb found at Tell Abraq measures 11 X 8.2 X .4 cm. Both sides of the comb bear identical, incised decoration in the form of two long-stemmed flowers with crenate or dentate leaves, flanking three dotted circles arranged in a triangular pattern. Bone and ivory combs with dotted-circle decoration are well-known in the Harappan area (e.g. at Chanhu-daro and Mohenjo-daro), but none of the Harappan combs bear the distinctive floral motif of the Tell Abraq comb. These flowers are identified as tulips, perhaps Mountain tulip or Boeotian tulip (both of which grow in Afghanistan) which have an undulate leaf. There is a possibility that the comb is an import from Bactria, perhaps transmitted through Meluhha to the Oman Peninsula site of Tell Abraq. Tell Abraq comb and axe with epigraph.[41]

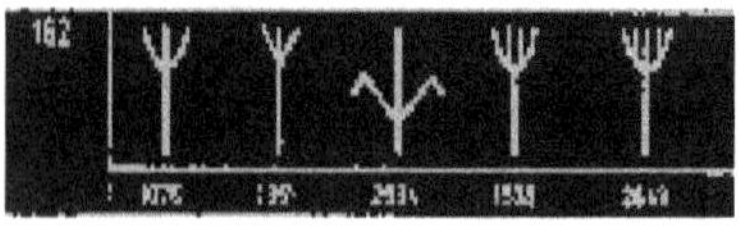

The sign on this potsherd (with five petals as in *tabernae montana, tagaraka*) is stylized as Sign 162 (with three prongs) and Sign 165 (with five petals). Sign 167 shows five petals (and variants show many more branches). The sign also is ligatured to form other signs:

Seal impression from Harappa (Kenoyer, 1998); a woman is carrying a three-petalled flower.

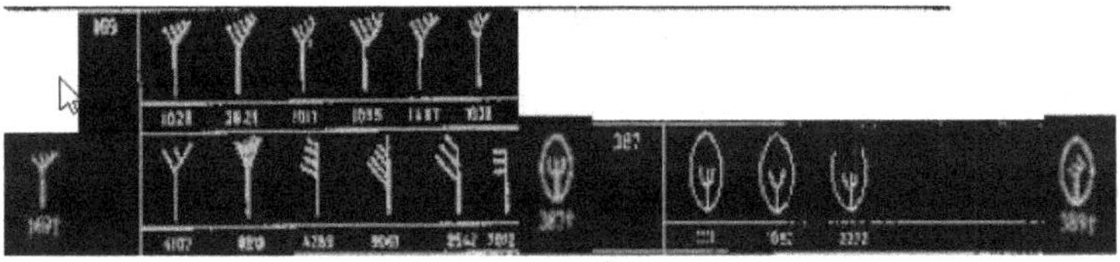

A number of glyph variants are used in texts. pajhaṛ 'to sprout from a root' Rebus: pasra 'smithy'.

Tree in front. Fish inl front of and above a one-horned bull. Cylinder seal impression (IM 8028). Ur. Mesopotamia. White shell. 1.7 cm. high, dia. 0.9 cm.

"No.7…a bull, unhumpd, of th so-alled 'unicorn' type, raises his head towards a simplified version of a tree, and two uncertain objects, one a sort of trefoil, are shown above his back. Under his head is an unmistakable character of the Indus script, the 'fish' with cross-hatchings…"[42] This is a good example of Meluhhans at work in Ur, which was evolving a tradition of veneration of the tree as a sacred symbol of a supreme divinity, in one case, *Shamash* (Akkadian or synonym, *Utu* of Sumerian).

The Sumerian sun-god was known as Utu. In the early hymn "Enki and the World Order" Utu is depicted as a powerful bull: "The valiant Utu, the bull who stands secure, who proudly displays his power, the father of the great city, the place where the sun rises."[43]

In the context of Indus writing, the 'bull' hieroglyph relates to a smith. Further researches are needed to explain the Bull-man hieroglyphs on Sumer-Elam-Mesopotamia artifacts, starting with a hypothesis that such a hieroglyphic depiction may relate to the work in smithy-forge of the bronze-age.

Mohenjo-daro Seal. m1180a .Text1303 Human-faced

markhor. In front is a stylized tree. *kuṭi* 'tree' Rebus: *kuṭhi* 'smelter'. *mũh* 'face'; rebus: metal ingot (Santali) *mũhã* = the quantity of iron produced at one time in a native smelting furnace of the Kolhes; iron produced by the Kolhes and formed like a four-cornered piece a little pointed at each end (Santali) *dhaṭu* ,*dhaṭhu*) 'scarf' (WPah.) Rebus: *dhātu* 'mineral' (Sanskrit), *dhatu* id. (Santali). *miṇḍhāl* 'markhor' (Torwali) Rebus: *mẽṛhẽt, meḍ* 'iron' *ispat mẽṛhẽt* 'steel' (Munda. Santali). The smithy catalog thus includes: smelter, mineral ores, iron working.

Scene of Libation to the God Shamash

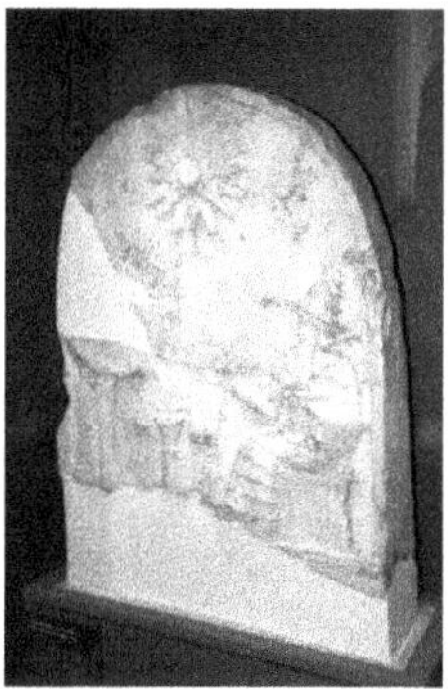

Sb 7 Richelieu room 3 Louvre Museum. A sovereign pours libation on an altar before a seated god, recognisable by his tiara (crown) with several rows of horns.

The god holds a ring and a rod, symbols of power and justice. A rayed sun disc dominates the scene. These symbols are often associated with Shamash, sun-god but also god of justice. The symbolism in the Bible is identical.[44]

Votive bas-relief - Libation offered to a vegetation goddess.

Twig, overflowing water as hieroglyphs

Old Babylonian Lady with Flowing Vases

Mesopotamia; Old Babylonian Period, 1800-1600 BC; Height 3.9 inches

A mold-made, tan terracotta plaque in raised relief shows a standing female figure with a long flounced dress as the Lady of the Flowing Vases. This individual, known from an almost life-size statue found at Mari, is associated with the source of the pure waters, and the god of fresh waters, Ea. She holds two vases, one in each hand at her stomach. Two streams of fresh water flow from the vases, one to the right and one to the left, then down into two other vases placed at her sides. She has a full hairdo with no divine crown.[45]

Bas-relief representing the mid-Assyrian god Ashur

feeding two goats, two goddesses with vases of overflowing water near his feet, discovered and stored in the Ancient Assyrian Museum -Vorderasiatisches Museum de Berlin.

Rebus readings:

lo 'pot to overflow'[46] *kāṇḍa* 'water'.

Rebus: लोखंड *lokhaṇḍ* Iron tools, vessels, or articles in

general.

kūtī = bunch of twigs (Sanskrit)

kuṭhi 'smelting furnace' (Santali)

The drama of the new year: the seal of the scribe Zaganita.

Glyptic use of tree in ancient India from the bronze-age

Glyph *khōṇḍa*: 'broken tree branch': *khōṇḍa* A tree of which the head and branches are broken off, a stock or stump: also the lower portion of the trunk—that below the branches. (Marathi) Allograph: खोंड [*khōṇḍa*] *m* A young bull, a bullcalf (Marathi). Rebus: *kõdā* 'to turn in a lathe' (Bengali)

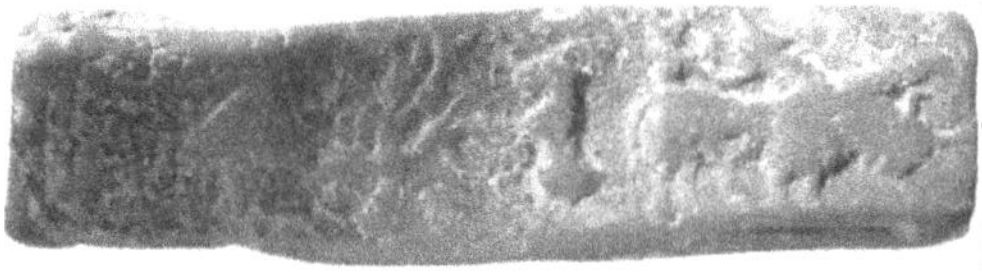

Mohenjo-daro tablet. m1430C, body of bison, three heads: bison, antelope, bull; a pair of goat(s), tree branch

Zebu and twig with leaves. In front of the standard device and stylizd tree of 9 leaves are the black buck antelopes. Black paint on red ware of Kulli style. Mehi. 2nd half of 3rd millennium BCE.[47]

Mohenjo-daro tablet.m1431E (Drilling, goats+tree) From R.—a person holding a vessel; a woman with a platter (?); a

kneeling person with a staff in his hands facing the woman; a goat with its forelegs on a platform under a tree. [Or, two antelopes flanking a tree on a platform, with one antelope looking backwards?]

-- kuṭi 'tree'; mlekh 'goat'; rebus: milakkhu 'copper' (Pali)

Sumerian cylinder seal showing flanking goats with hooves on tree and/or mountain. Uruk period. (After Joyce Burstein in: Katherine Anne Harper, Robert L. Brown, 2002, The roots of tantra, SUNY Press, p.100) After Amiet,

P., 1961, *La glyptique mesopotamienne archaique*, Paris: 497; Mundigak IV.3; 3. Ka. kōḍu horn, tusk, branch of a tree; *Ta.* kōṭu summit of a hill, peak, mountain Rebus: खोट [khōṭa] *f* A mass of metal (unwrought or of old metal melted down); an ingot or wedge. Hence खोटसाळ [khōṭasāḷa] *a* (खोट & साळ from शाला) Alloyed--a metal. (Marathi) loa = a species of fig tree, ficus glomerata, the fruit of *ficus glomerata* (Santali) Rebus: lo 'iron' (Assamese, Bengali); loa 'iron' (Gypsy); loh 'metal' (Skt.); lo 'copper'. Leaf on mountain: kamaṛkom 'petiole of leaf'; rebus: kampaṭṭam 'mint'. *daṭhi, daṭi* the petioles and mid-ribs of a compound leaf after the leaflets have been plucked off, stalks of certain plants, as Indian corn, after the grain has been taken off (Santali) Rebus: dhatu 'mineral.

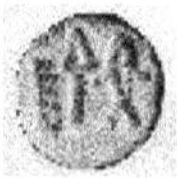

h243Ah243B Harappa Tablet in bas-relief eraka 'nave of wheel' Rebus: eraka, era, erka 'copper, weapons' (Kannada). loa 'ficus' Rebus: lo 'copper'.

Kotdiji burial shard showing leaf. Loa 'ficus' Rebus: lo 'copper'.

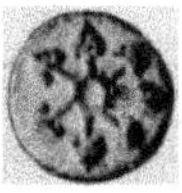

Bulls and bull-men flank a mountain topped by a leaf. Interpreted as scene representing

Gilgamesh and Ea-bani in conflict with bulls in a wooded and mountainous country. Cylinder seal impression.Mesopotamia. British Museum No. 89308. *ḍhangar* 'bull' Rebus: *dhangar* 'blacksmith' (Maithili) *ḍangar* 'blacksmith' (Hindi) *loa* 'ficus' Rebus: *lo* 'copper'.

Kalibangan053 Sign 232 ṭākuro = hill top (N.); ṭāngī = hill, stony country (Or.); ṭāngara = rocky hilly land (Or.); ḍāngā = hill, dry upland (B.); ḍāg mountain-ridge (H.)(CDIAL 5476). Rebus: ḍānro = a term of contempt for a blacksmith (N.)(CDIAL

5524). ṭhākur = blacksmith (Mth.) (CDIAL 5488). Damgar ‘merchant’ (Akkadian)

Cylinder seal impression. 2250-2150 BCE.Mesopotamia. Chert. Ht. 1 1/16 in. (2.8 cm). The seal depicts a man hunting a markhor in a mountain forest. The owner of the seal was Balu-illi, a high court official whose title was ‘cupbearer’[48] *miṇḍhāl* ‘markhor’ (Torwali) Rebus: *mẽṛhẽt, meḍ* ‘iron’ *ispat mẽṛhẽt* ‘steel’ (Munda. Santali) *kūṭamu* ‘summit of a mountain’ (Telugu) Rebus: *kūṭakamu* ‘mixture’ (Telugu) *kūṭam* ‘workshop’ (Tamil) The Sign 230 thus connotes a workshop for an alloyed metal, kūṭa [e.g. copper + dhatu ‘mineral (ore)’ as in: ārakūṭa = brass (Sanskrit)]

Ur. Shell plaque. Shell plaque From Ur, Southern Iraq (c. 2,600-2,400 B.C.) Entwined in the branches of a flowering tree, two goats appear to be nibbling on its leaves. This decorative plaque, which was carved from shell and highlighted with bitumen, was also excavated from the Royal Tombs of Ur. The glyphics on this plaque are comparable to the glyphics on Tablet 1431E showing two goat glyphs flanking a tree glyph. Mlekh, mr̤eka 'goat' (Br.Telugu); rebus: milakkhu 'copper'. डगर [ḍagara] A slope or ascent (as of a river's bank, of a small hill). A pair is dula; rebus: dul 'cast (metal)'(Santali)Rebus: ḍāṅgar 'blacksmith' (H.) Alternative: damgar 'merchant' (Akkadian). Thus, the glyptic composition is read rebus: dul mlekh ḍāṅgar 'cast copper-smith'.

Harappa tablet: h95-2485 sides 1 and 2. Harvard Harappa Project. A person stands below a stylized arch adorned with ficus leaves and ending in volutes typical on Mesopotamian cylinder seals and

artifacts. He has a twig on his head and wears a pigtail, 'scarf' glyph. The bunch of twigs = *kūdī, kūṭī* (Sanskrit) *kūdī* (also written as kūṭī in manuscripts) occurs in the

Atharvaveda (AV 5.19.12) and Kauśika Sūtra[49] denotes it as a twig. This is identified as that of Badari, the jujube tied to the body of the dead to efface their traces.[50] Rebus: *kuṭhi* 'a furnace for smelting iron ore to smelt iron'; *kolheko kuṭhieda* 'koles smelt iron'. (Santali)

Glyphic composition on a Mohenjo-daro tablet.

maṇḍhwa, maṇḍua, maṇḍwa 'a temporary shed or booth erected on the occasion of a marriage' (Santali) maṇḍā 'warehouse, workshop' (Konkani). loa 'ficus' Rebus: lo 'copper'.

Details of the tiger + spy + leafless tree glyphics are clearly seen on a Mohenjodaro seal m0309. hēraka --, *°rika* -- m. 'spy'. Glyphics read rebus: *kol kammara* 'iron smith' [*kola* 'tiger' (Telugu); *krammaru* 'head turned

back' (Telugu)]; *eraka* 'copper' [*heraka* 'spy']; *kõdār* 'turner' (Bengali) [*khōṇḍa* 'leafless tree' (Marathi).] Rebus: *koṇḍ* 'turning on a lathe'.

Harappa tablet. Mold made. Faience. H2000-4483/2342-01 HARP. Was found in the eroded levels of the tablet workshop in Trench 54. One one side is a short iscription under a rectangular box filled with 24 dots (or, a pair of 12 dots). The reverse narrates two bulls face to face under a thorny or leafless tree. *paṭṭa* 'slab, tablet' Rebus: *paṭṭarai* 'community, smiths' workplace'. Leaf-shaped: *pathar, patras* 'leaf' (Kashmiri).Rebus: *pattar* 'guild (of smiths)'; *pattar, vartaka* 'merchants'. *khōṇḍa* 'leafless tree' (Marathi) Rebus: *koṇḍ* 'turning on a lathe'. *kõdār* 'turner' (Bengali) ḍangar 'bull' ḍāṅgar 'cattle'; rebus: ḍhangar blacksmith'; *ṭhākur* ' blacksmith ' (Maithili)

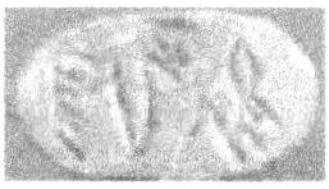

dula 'pair' Rebus: dul 'cast (metal). The three glyphs are a frequently occurring sequence on Indus writing

corpora.This set together with the fish ligatured with a ^ (superfixed). On the text of the tablet.

The twelve notches or indentations on the rectangular slab: *pattu* 'twelve'? (counting on 12 digits of four

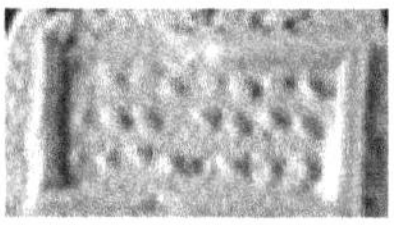

fingers excluding the thumb); thus *dul-pattu* may denote cast (metal) *paṭṭarai* 'smiths' workplace'. खांडा [*khāṇḍā*] *m* a jag, notch, or indentation (as upon the edge of a tool or weapon); rebus: *khāṇḍā* 'metal tools, pots and pans'. Thus, 24 indentations on the cartouche may read rebus *dul-pattu khāṇḍā* 'cast metal tools/weapons of smiths' guild' of *kõdār* 'turners who work on a lathe'. This tablet is a catalog of a smithy-forge.

Tree hieroglyph together with svastika hieroglyph

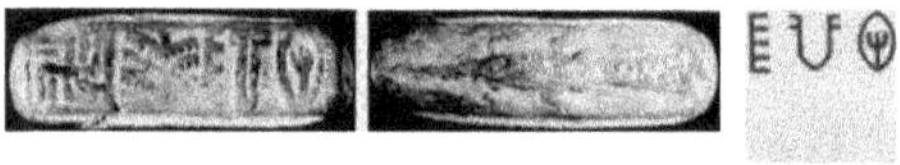

m0482At m0482Bt 1620: Gharial, with

a fish held in its jaw and/or surrounded by a school of fish. Svastika 'glyph' Rebus: sattva, jasta 'zinc'. khoṇḍa *'leafless tree; Rebus: kõdār* turner (a lathe-worker)'.

karā 'crocodile' Rebus: karā 'artisan'. Ayo 'fish' Rebus: ayo 'metal, iron'.

Tree and three other hieroglyphs occur on Sohgaura copper plate of ca. 6th century BCE[51], which also includes a Brahmi inscription about two warehouse facilities for itinerant artisans. Two *koṣṭhāgāra* (*dvāra koṭṭhaka*) attached with *kuṭi* 'tree' Rebus: *kuṭhi* 'smelters' and *kūṭa* 'mountain summit' Rebus: *kūṭa* 'workshop' *khaṇḍa* 'arrow' Rebus: *khaṇḍā* 'tools, pots and pans'. The Brahmi text is consistent with these rebus readings of the hieroglyphs.

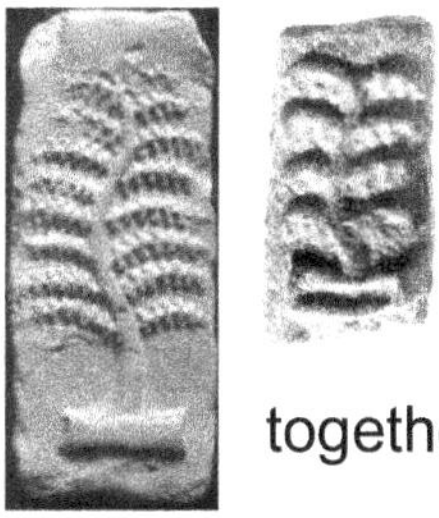

h728 One side of Harappa tablet. Leafless tree on ingot. Harappa tablet. The 'tree' hieroglyph, together with hieroglyphs of elephant, svastika continues to be used in the historical periods on punch-marked and cast coins of many mints across a vast area from Takshasila (Afghanistan) to Karur (South India) and Sri Lanka with or without syllabic inscriptions using kharoṣṭī and brāhmī scripts from ca. 6th century BCE.

Kuninda copper coin. Ca. 3rd century BCE. Hieroglyphs: tree on platform; mountain-summit; svastika; portable furnace; bull; naked woman; liquid measure; paired fish-tails as śrivatsa; dotted circle. Some rebus readings: 1. kol 'furnace, forge' (Kuwi), *kol* working in iron, blacksmith (Tamil); 2. satthiya 'zinc', jasta 'zinc' (Kashmiri), satva, 'zinc' (Pkt.); 3. खोट [*khōṭa*] *f* 'A mass of metal (unwrought or of old metal melted down); an ingot or wedge' (Kashmiri); *khoṭā* ' alloyed' (Marathi) 4. *kuṭi* 'smelter furnace'; 5. *sangada* 'guild' ; 6. *khóṛnõ* 'to dig, scratch, engrave' (Western Pahari).

Sacred tree hieroglyph

kuṭi 'tree' is used on many Indus writing artifacts to denote a key resource of a smithy/forge in bronze-age metallurgy: 'smelter furnace'. kuṭi, kuṭhi, kuṭa, kuṭha a tree (Kaus'.); kuḍa tree (Pkt.); kuṛā tree; kaṛek tree, oak (Pas;.)(CDIAL 3228). kuṭha, kuṭa (Ka.), kudal (Go.) kudar. (Go.) kuṭhāra, kuṭha, kuṭaka = a tree

(Sanskrit) kut., kurun: = stump of a tree (Bond.a); khuṭ = id. (Or.) kuṭamu = a tree (Telugu) Rebus: *kuṭhi, kuṭi* (Or.; Sad. *koṭhi*) (1) the smelting furnace of the blacksmith; kuṭire bica duljaḍko talkena, they were feeding the furnace with ore (Santali) kuṭhi-o of a smelting furnace, to be made; the smelting furnace of the blacksmith is made of mud, cone-shaped, 2' 6" dia. At the base and 1' 6" at the top. The hole in the centre, into which the mixture of charcoal and iron ore is poured, is about 6" to 7" in dia. At the base it has two holes, a smaller one into which the nozzle of the bellow is inserted, as seen in fig. 1, and a larger one on the opposite side through which the molten iron flows out into a cavity (Mundari) kuṭhi = an earthen furnace for smelting iron; make do., smelt iron; *kolheko do kuṭhi benaokate baliko dhukana*, the Kolhes build an earthen furnace and smelt iron-ore, blowing the bellows; tehen:ko kuṭhi yet kana, they are working (or building) the furnace to-day (H. koṭhī) (Santali. Bodding)

Glyph 'leaf, petal': A 'leaf' glyph has to be distinguished from a 'petals' glyph because the leaf orthography is clearly representative of the *ficus* genus which attains sacredness in later historical periods in the Indian linguistic area.

Glyptic elements of m296 seal impression: 1. Two heads of one-horned young bulls; 2. ligatured to a pair of rings and a standard device; 3. ligatured to a precise count of nine leaves. Read rebus: koḍiyum 'heifer, rings on neck'; खोंड [khōṇḍa] m A young bull, a bullcalf. (Marathi) గోడ [gōda] gōda. [Tel.] n. An ox. A beast. kine, cattle.(Telugu) koḍiyum (G.) Rebus : B. kõdā 'to turn in a lathe'; Or. kūnda 'lathe', kũdibā, kūd 'to turn' (→ Drav. Kur. kūd 'lathe') (CDIAL 3295). Rebus: koḍ 'workshop' (Kuwi.G.); dula 'pair' (Kashmiri); rebus: dul 'cast metal' (Mu.) lo, no 'nine' (B.); loa 'ficus religiosa' (Santali); rebus: loh 'metal' (Skt.); loa 'copper' (Santali) sangaḍa 'jointed animals' (Marathi); sangaḍa 'lathe' (G.) Rebus: jaṅgaḍ 'entrusment articles'. Part of the pictorial motif is thus decoded rebus: loh dul koḍ 'metal cast(ing) smithy turner (lathe) workshop'. Part of the inscription is read rebus: *ayaskāṇḍa kole.l* 'smithy, excellent quantity of iron'.

The stem in the orthographic composition relates to 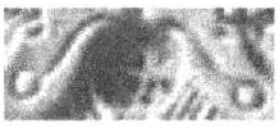 *sangaḍa* 'lathe/furnace' (yielding crucible stone ore nodules), the standard device which is depicted frequently in front of 'one-horned heifer'. Rebus: *sangāta* 'association, guild' or, *sangatarāsu* 'stone-cutter' (Telugu). The 'globules' glyphic joining the two ringed necks of a pair of one-horned heifers may connote: goṭi. It may connote a forge.

Glyph: 'piece'; the two rings emanating from the top of the portable furnace denote *khoṭā* 'forged'; *khoṭa* 'alloy': guḍá—1. — In sense 'fruit, kernel' cert. ← Drav., cf. Tam. koṭṭai 'nut, kernel'; A. goṭ 'a fruit, whole piece', °ṭā 'globular, solid', guṭi 'small ball, seed, kernel'; B. goṭā 'seed, bean, whole'; Or. goṭā 'whole, undivided', goṭi 'small ball, cocoon', goṭāli 'small round piece of chalk'; Bi. goṭā 'seed'; Mth. goṭa 'numerative particle' (CDIAL 4271) Rebus: *khoṭ* m. 'base, alloy' (Punjabi) Rebus: koṭe 'forging (metal)(Mu.) Rebus: goṭī f. 'lump of silver' (G.) goṭi = silver (G.) koḍ 'workshop' (G.). Glyph: 'two links in a chain': *kaḍī* a chain; a hook; a link (G.); *kaḍum* a bracelet, a ring

(G.) Rebus: *kaḍiyo* [Hem. Des. *kaḍaio* = Skt. *sthapati* a mason] a bricklayer; a mason; *kaḍiyaṇa, kaḍiyeṇa* a woman of the bricklayer caste; a wife of a bricklayer (G.) The stone-cutter is also a mason.

kamaḍha = *ficus religiosa* (Skt.); kamar.kom 'ficus' (Santali) rebus: kamaṭa = portable furnace for melting precious metals (Te.); kampaṭṭam = mint (Ta.) Vikalpa: Fig leaf 'loa'; rebus: loh '(copper) metal'. loha-kāra 'metalsmith' (Skt.).

The symbolism associated with the tree in the context of metalwork is integral to the sacredness associated with the word for a smithy, kole.l. The same word is used in Kota language to denote a temple. Thus, repertoire of tools, implements and resources used in a smithy or forge also get sacred associations in Indian tradition. A characteristic feature of āgama temple tradition is to arm icons of divinities in temples with multiple hands carrying multiple weapons and tools.

Safflower as a hieroglyph in Assyrian Tree of Life

This relief on the side of a cosmetic vessel from Nippur shows one of the many other depictions of goats in trees. *karaḍa* 'safflower' Rebus: *karaḍa* 'hard alloy'. tagara 'ram, antelope' Rebus: tagara 'tin'; damgar 'merchant'.

After Fig. 6.28 Gansell, 2008; Gold floral crown with female figures and grape clusters; Nimrud, Tomb III; 8th c.; diam. 24 cm. h. 16 cm; IM 115619[52]

Inanna's symbol is the eight-pointed star or rosette, appearing between the pincers of two scorpions on the square face of this stamp seal. Dated c.3300 BCE. North Mesopotamia. Akkadian princess, High Priestess of the Moon god

Nanna, daughter of Sargon the Great. c 2285–2250 BCE.

Found at Gonur-Tepe was a grand palace and temples with Zoroastrian fire-altars. An intriguing find was a gold trinket which resembles a symbol used on kudurru and ancient Susa-Elam-Mesopotamian cylinder seals.

Pink chalcedony cylinder seal. Mesopotamia. Kassite dynasty, about 1400-1300 BCE. Shamash seated before a 'sun' disc and an 'fire-altar' symbol.

This cylinder seal is typical of the period when the dynasty of Kassite kings (probably originally from eastern Mesopotamia) ruled Babylonia (about 1550-1155 BC).

The seven-line cuneiform inscription, a prayer to Shamash, can be translated: 'Shamash, king of heaven and earth whose *me*'s are brilliant, who advances with horns, who - through his (servant) who reveres him - has brought salvation: Sha-ilimma-damqa, son of Lugal-mansi.' Shamash represents the brilliant light of the sun, which returns every day to illuminate the life of mankind, as well as giving beneficial warmth, which causes plants to grow. In Akkadian tradition he was sometimes the son of the god of heaven Anu or of the supreme god Enlil. His principal temple was called E-babbar ('White House') at Sippar. Presumably because the sun, in its path across the skies, see everything, Shamash came to be regarded as the god of truth, justice and right. As a protector and destroyer of evil, he also acted as a warrior. The *me's* referred to in the quotation are properties of the gods which enable many activities, central to civilized human life, to take place: such as religion, kingship, ritual music. This is a very fundamental concept in Sumerian religion.[53]

karaḍa -- m. 'safflower', *°ḍā* -- f. ' a tree like the karañja ' (Prakrit); M. *karḍī*, *°ḍaī* f. ' safflower, Carthamus tinctorius and its seed '. (CDIAL 2788). *karaṭataila ' oil of safflower '. M. *karḍel* n. ' oil from the seed of safflower '.(CDIAL

2789). Rebus: करड्याची अवटी [karaḍyācī avaṭī] *f* An implement of the goldsmith. A stamp for forming the bars or raised lines called करडा. It is channeled or grooved with (or without) little cavities. करडा [karaḍā] *m* The arrangement of bars or embossed lines (plain or fretted with little knobs) raised upon a तार of gold by pressing and driving it upon the अवटी or grooved stamp. Such तार is used for the ornament बुगडी, for the hilt of a पट्टा or other sword &c. Applied also to any similar barform or line-form arrangement (pectination) whether embossed or indented; as the edging of a rupee &c. करडणें or करंडणें [karaḍaṇē or ṅkaraṇḍaṇēṃ] *v c* To gnaw or nibble; to wear away by biting (Marathi). Rebus: करडा [*karaḍā*] Hard from alloy--iron, silver &c. (Marathi) *kharādī*' turner, a person who fashions or shapes objects on a lathe' (Gujarati)

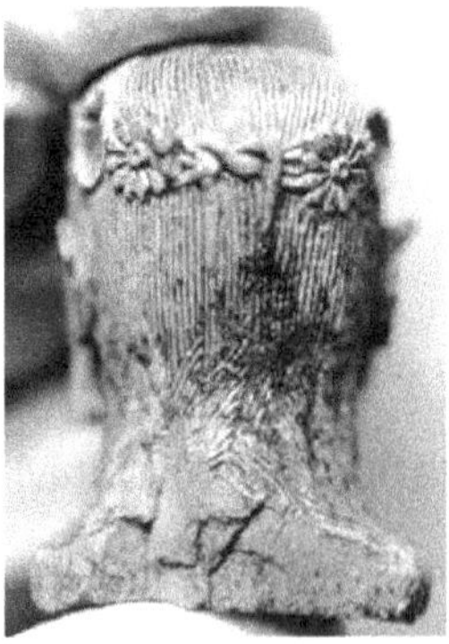

After Fig. 3.14, Gansell 2008; Ivory sculpture in the round of a female with braids and a crown, rear view; Nimrud; 9th-8th c.; h. 5 cm: BM 118237.[54]

After Fig. 5.27, Gansell 2008; Basalt female caryatid, detail of the neck and chest; Tell Halaf; 9th c.; full h. of sculpture 274 cm.; Aleppo, museum number not known (Moortgat 1955, pl. 135).

Cultivated representative of the genus *Carthamus* is *Carthamus tinctorius* L. (safflower). "Safflower appears first in a number of early Bronze Age (3000 BCE) sites in northern and central Syria...The Near Eastern Bronze Age evidence shows striking exclusiveness in the distribution patterns of safflower and flax, with flax being restricted to Levantine and Iranian sites...At the same time the geographically complementary evidence may indicate a similar use of the two crops and most probably suggests that the safflower was also used for oil almost from the beginning of its cultivation...Recent genetic studies suggest that *C. palaestinus*, a wild species restricted to the deserts of southern Israel and western Iraq is the progenitor of *C. tinctorius*..."[55]

"An interesting source for the use of a wide variety of garden vegetables is afforded by a unique tablet in the British Museum bearing two columns of entries on either side in which Akkadian names of no fewer than sixty-one plants grown in the garden of Merodach-Baladan are enumerated...the text lists dill (Anetbum graveolens, Akk. sibetum), mjnt (ninu), safflower or 'bastard saffron' (Carthamus tinctorius, Akk. azlsupiru), coriander (kisibirru), thyme (Thymus, Akk. zambu.ru), hyssop (Hyssopus, Akk. ziipu), and asafoetida (Ferula asafoetida, Akk. surbi)..."[56]

Pine-cone as a hieroglyph

Personnage tenant un ibex et une

fleur de pavot - Assyrie | Site officiel du musée du Louvre. Person holding an ibex and a poppy flower (pine-cone?) Low-relief from the m wall of king Sargon II's palace at Dur Sharrukin in Assyria (now Khorsabad in Iraq), c. 713–716 BC. From Paul-Émile Botta's excavations in 1843–1844.

tagara 'ram, goat' Rebus: damgar 'merchant'.

Source: Image of Aleppo pine cone (Israel)[57]

Ash. piċ -- kandə ' pine ', Kt. pṳ̄ċi, piċi, Wg. puċ, püċ (pṳ̄ċ -- kəŕ ' pine -- cone '), Pr. wyoċ, Shum. lyēwič (lyē -- ?).(CDIAL 8407). Cf. Gk. peu/kh f. ' pine ', Lith. pušìs, OPruss. peuse NTS xiii 229. The suffix –kande in the lexeme: Ash. piċ-- kandə ' pine ' may be cognate with the bulbous glyphic related to a mangrove root: Koḍ. kaṇḍe root-stock from which small roots grow; ila·ti kaṇḍe sweet potato (ila·ti England). Tu. kaṇḍe, gaḍḍè a bulbous root; Ta. kaṇṭal mangrove, Rhizophora mucronata; dichotomous mangrove, Kandolia rhoodii. Ma. kaṇṭa bulbous root as of lotus, plantain; point where branches and bunches grow out of the stem of a palm; kaṇṭal what is bulb-like, half-ripe jackfruit and other green fruits; R. candel. (DEDR 1171). Rebus: *kaṇḍa* 'tools, pots and pans of metal'.

A cylinder seal impression. *āra* 'serpent' Rebus: *āra* 'brass'. *kandə* 'pine' Rebus: *kaṇḍa* 'tools, pots and pans of metal'.

Sumerian Mother-of-Pearl Inlay: a Bald-Headed Priest leading a Bull[58]

Mesopotamia; circa 2500 BC; Height 1.5 inches

The square plaque made for inlay into furniture or, perhaps, a musical instrument is incised with the figure of a standing bald-headed priest walking to the right and leading a long-horned bull. The priest grasps the bull by its head. Perhaps a ritual scene in a temple is represented here. Four large unopened floral buds decorate the background. A finely executed miniature artwork, this was once part of a luxury item. The original pearl, pink and turquoise colors of the mother-of-pearl shell are still vibrant.

Mesopotamian lapis lazuli cylinder seal in the British Museum. Early Dynastic Period, about 2600-2400 BCEUpper register: two bearded human-headed bulls guarding the sacred plant. Anzu-Imdugud bird attacks. Cerubim flank the scene: one on the left has a long-tailed animal's lower body, while the one on the right has a human body but a bird-like head. Lower register: antelope or goat, antlered stag, eagle.

Kui gunda (gundi-) to sprout, bud, shoot forth into bud or ear; *n.* a sprouting, budding. ? *Kuwi* (Isr.) kunda a very small plot of ground (e.g. for seed-bed). *Kur.* kundnā to germinate, bud, shoot out; kundrnā to be born; kundrkā birth; kundrta'ānā to generate, beget, produce. *Malt.* kunde to be born, be created.(DEDR 1729). Rebus: kunda ‘to turn in a lathe’. pajhaṛ ‘kite’ Rebus: pasra ‘smithy’. *karaḍa* ‘duck’ Rebus: *karaḍa* 'hard alloy' *kalāda* ‘goldsmith workshop’.

Cylinder seal: bull-man, bearded hero, and lion contest frieze

Period: Early Dynastic III Date: ca. 2600–2350 BCE

Geography: Mesopotamia Culture: Sumerian.

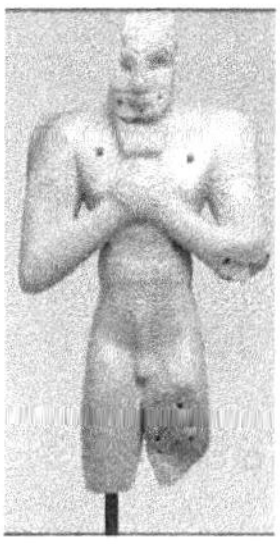

Medium: Marble Dimensions: 1.75 in. (4.45 cm) Classification: Stone-Cylinder Seals Credit Line: Gift of Walter Hauser, 1955 Accession Number: 55.65.4 Met Museum.

karā 'crocodile' (Santali) Rebus: *karāvu* 'artisan, smith'.

Alabaster bull-man. Tell Djokha. Early Dynastic II-III, ca. mid-3rd millennium B.C.E. Height: 34.8 cm. Sumerian Miniature Brown Serpentine Sculpture of a Human-headed Bull. Mesopotamia; circa 2100 BC; Length 1.75 inches. Two views

The human face portrays a man with strong, almost regal facial features including a large curved Semitic nose, a full mouth, finely formed eyes with eyebrows that meet at the bridge of his nose and bull's ears. He has a long curled beard, large ringlets of hair reaching down each side of his face almost to the end of his beard and two single horns curved forward at the top of his forehead. His horns indicate that he is a deity. The mythological animal is seated with his legs and tail tucked under him. He has finely engraved hair on the back of his head and on his hindquarters. The bull's erect phallus is visible on the underside of the sculpture. A wonderfully executed, rare and perfectly preserved miniature work of art by one of the finest Sumerian miniature carvers.[59]

Statuette of an androcephalous bull. Neo-Sumerian period. Chlorite with inlays H. 12.10 cm; W. 14.90 cm; D. 8 cm Acquired in 1898 AO 2752 Louvre Museum

[quote] **The human-headed bull.**
The animal is shown lying, its head turned to the side and its tail underneath its right hoof. On its head is the divine headdress with three pairs of horns. It has a man's face with large elongated eyes, a beard covering half its cheeks and joining with the mustache before cascading down over its breast, where it ends in small curls, and long ringlets framing its face. The ears, however, are a bull's, though fleecy areas at the shoulders and hindquarters seem to suggest the animal is actually a bison. Another example in the Louvre displays particularly fine workmanship, the

eyes and the whole body being enriched with decorative elements, applied or inlaid in trilobate and lozenge-shaped cavities (in the hooves). There is a small group of these recumbent bulls dating from the Neo-Sumerian period (around 2150-2000 BC), one of which is inscribed with the name of Gudea, the Second Dynasty ruler of Lagash. In the Neo-Assyrian period (9th-6th centuries BC), the human-headed bull, now with a pair of wings, becomes the guardian of the royal palace, flanking the doors through which visitors entered. This creature was a lamassu, a benevolent protective spirit generally associated with the sun-god Shamash.

A base for a vessel, or for a statue of a deity?

An elongated cavity of irregular shape in the middle of the back of this statuette, also found in other examples, might have been intended to hold a removable offering bowl, as illustrated in Mesopotamian iconography. The Louvre has a statuette of a dog from Telloh, inscribed with the name of Sumu-ilum, king of Larsa in the 19th century

BC, which has a mortice in the back into which fits an unpolished tenon supporting a small oval cup. It may be that the statuette was subsequently adapted to this use. Relief depictions also show a seated deity (usually the sun-god Shamash) with his foot on the back of a similar hybrid creature, which might suggest that they served as bases for statuettes of gods. Another statuette of a recumbent human-headed bull has two horizontal perforations in the narrower forequarters, suggesting that these might have served to attach a small lid.

Steatite: a popular stone in the reign of Gudea

Steatite, the soft stone used for this statuette, was the material frequently chosen in the reign of Gudea to make precious objects connected with cultic rituals, such as libation vessels and offering dishes. Statuettes representing worshippers were also carved from this stone, generally depicting members of the royal family, such as the statuette of a woman with a scarf, or high-ranking dignitaries.[unquote][60]

Part of a Sumerian seal from about 2000 BC. Rohl ,1998 inteprets the bull-man as Gilgamesh (Rohl,p170), but the bull-man image goes back to much earlier times.

A lamassu from Khorsabad (Louvre)... protective deity

with a bull's body, eagle's wings, and a human head. “The Sumerian word *lama*, which is rendered in Akkadian as *lamassu*, refers to a protective deity, who is usually female. She is often represented as a standing figure that introduces guests to another, superior god. So she is actually a servant. Her male counterpart is called *alad* or, in Akkadian, *šêdu*...However, there are Greek coins that show lamassu's, like those of the Sicilian cities of Gela and Panormus. The latter, modern Palermo, may, as a

Phoenician colony, have had artistic ties with the east."

A bull-man on a coin from Gela (Bode-Museum, Berlin).[61]

"War"-panel of the Standard of Ur, ca. 2600 BC, showing parading men, animals and chariots.

One hieroglyph on this Ur standard is a person holding a lyre. Glyph: *tambura* 'harp';

Rebus: *tambra* 'copper' (Pkt. Santali)

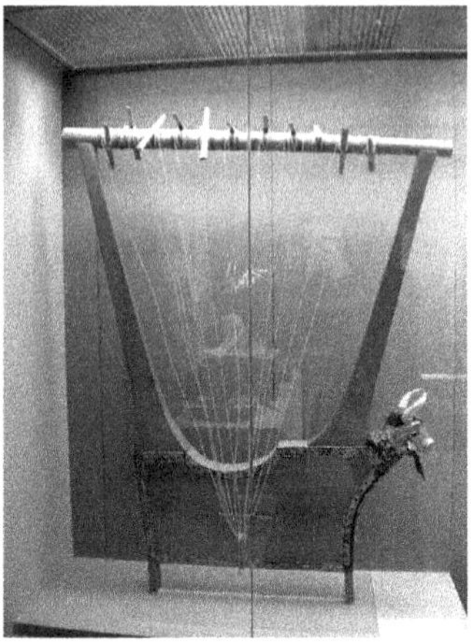

Detail from front panel

The front panel, partially under the beard, shows a nearly nude bearded male figure holding two rearing human-headed bulls in the top section, and below are three ritualistic scenes from a funeral banquet: a butchering hyena, an ass playing a lyre, and a scorpion-man. The combination of human and animal features are religious in nature.[62]

[quote]"Bull-headed Lyre" (Head Height: 35.6 cm; Plaque Height: 33 cm) from the Woolley-coined "King's Grave" royal tomb of Private Grave (PG) 789, constructed with gold, silver, lapis lazuli, shell, bitumen and wood, ca 2550 BCE at Ur. The lyre's panel depicts a hero grasping animals and animals acting like humans—serving at a banquet and playing music typically associated with banquets. The bottom panel shows a scorpion-man and a gazelle with human features. The scorpion-man is a creature associated with the mountains of sunrise and sunset, distant lands of wild animals and demons, a place passed by the dead on their way to the Netherworld. [unquote][63]

Bull Man Protecting Horned Animals Attacked Felines; Scorpion Above Crossed Felines Cylinder seal and impression Mesopotamia, Early Dynastic III period (ca. 2600–2334 BCE) Marble 41 x 25 mm Seal no. 75[64]

A MESOPOTAMIAN INLAID MARBLE CALF LATE URUK-JEMDET NASR PERIOD, CIRCA 3300-2900 B.C.

Reclining with its legs folded under, the tail curled behind its right hind leg, the tapering head held square, with a downturned mouth, budding horns and triangular ears, the almond-shaped eyes inlaid in white stone, the lids in lapis lazuli, the pupils in dark material, heavy folds for the brows above, the body ornamented throughout with trilobate lapis lazuli inlays, the underside with a rectangular recess 4 1/8 in. (10.5 cm.) long. Provenance with Dr. Elie Borowski.Ludwig Herinek, Vienna, 1965.Lot Notes Many finely-sculpted figures of animals were found together in the Eanna temple precinct at Uruk Level III. Martin informs (p. 16 in Aruz, ed., Art of the First Cities, The Third Millennium B.C. from the Mediterranean to the Indus) that "the figures were apparently votive offerings to the goddess Inanna to ensure her continuing goodwill." For a similar example now in the Staatliche Museen zu Berlin, see no. 2b, pp. 16-17, op. cit. For a discussion of the type see ch. 1 in Behm-Blancke, Das Tierbild in der Altmesopotamischen Rundplastik.[65]

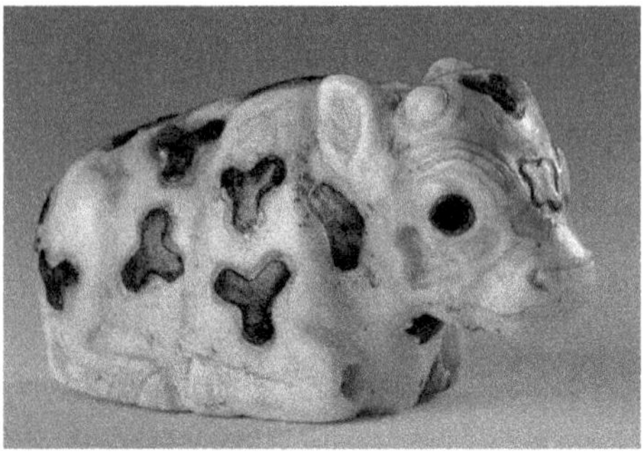

Limestone and lapis (l. 5.2cm), 3300-2900BC. Berlin, VA 14536 *Art of the First Cities* 2b

ISHTAR'S "MAGIC WAND

Notice how this all configures to be the same deity. In "The Lesser Key of Solomon", he is referred to as a very powerful demon. Depicted as a nude man with

feathered wings, wearing a crown, holding a serpent in one hand, and riding a dragon-like beast with

wings and a serpent-like tail. Considered to be a demon in the First Hierarchy and rules over 40 legions of Spirits.

On left is likely depiction of Inanna on a fragment of votive plaque

(Photographic credit: Julia M. Asher-Greve), from Nippur, Early Dynastic III Period (2047-1940 BCE); on right is likely depiction of Inanna - 87 mm tall gypsum statue from Sumerian Dynastic Period circa 2300-2000 BCE.[66]

Ishtar (pronounced /ˈɪʃtɑːr/; Transliteration: D*IŠTAR*; Akkadian: 𒀭𒈹) is the East Semitic Akkadian, Assyrian and Babylonian goddess of fertility, war, love, and sex. She is the counterpart to the Sumerian Inanna, and is the cognate for the Northwest Semitic Aramean goddess Astarte.[67]

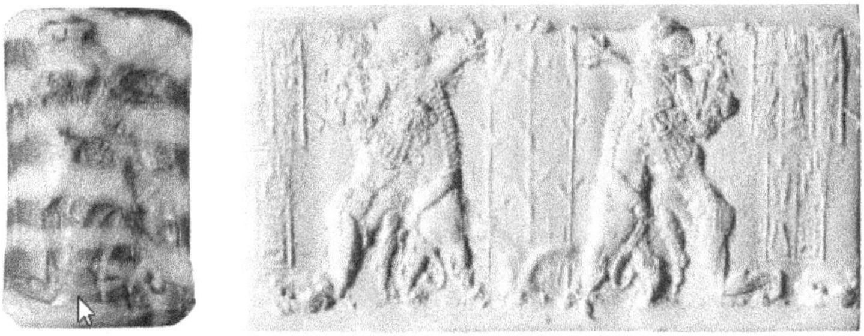

Figure 1.5 Gilgamesh Fighting a Lion. Ca. 2500–2000 B.C. Cylinder seal (left) and modern impression of a cylinder seal (right). British Museum. *The separate scenes, rolled out on this impression from the seal, which is about 1 inch high, depict the Sumerian hero in one of his many battles against beasts. The artist heightens the intensity of the physical struggle by placing Gilgamesh, with his legs bent and arms locked around the lion, at a sharp angle under the animal to muster his brute strength against his foe.*

Vorderasiatisches Museum (Near East Museum),

Berlin Tukulti-Ninurta I (meaning: "my trust is in [the warrior god] Ninurta"; reigned 1243–1207 BC) was a king of Assyria during the Middle Assyrian Empire (1366 - 1050 BC).

Sacred altar of Tukulti-Ninurta I

Cult pedestal of Tukulti-Ninurta I (1244-1207), Ishtar temple, Assur, Middle Assyrian period.[68] Altar with king Tukulti-Ninurta I The altar of Tukulti-Ninurta is an alabaster monument, carved in relief, measues 22 11/16 in. height, 22 11/16 in width. Discovered in the city of Assur (Qal'at Sherqat) in Ishtar Temple, built by Middle Assyrian King Tukulti-Ninurta I (1243-1207 BCE). On a semicircular projection at either end of its upper part, a thirteen-petalled rosette is carved. Tukulti-Ninurta approaches and kneels in front of the altar which has a vertical stick placed at its center. An Akkadian inscription notes dedication of the pedestal by Tikulti-Ninurta to god Nuṣku. "Cult platform of the god Nuṣku, chief vizier (Sukkalmah) of Ekur, bearer of the just scepter (nasi), courtier of the gods Assur and Enlil, who daily repeats the prayers of Tukulti-Ninurta, the king, his beloved, in the presence of the gods Assur and Enlil and a destiny of power (for him) withi ekur...may he (pronounce...the god Ass)ur, (my) lord, ...forever..." Ekur is a temple in Babylonia, the bond between heaven and earth.[69]

Another altar from Pyrennes

It has been suggested that some of the glyphs deployed on Mesopotamian artifacts/cylinder seals may be explained rebus using Meluhha (Mleccha) glosses. For example, the following altar which deploys 'fish' and 'svastika' hieroglyphs:

Altar, Pyrenees (South of France). I Century BCE (The altar shows a svastika and a fish – both are Sarasvati hieroglyphs of Indus writing.) *ayo* 'fish' Rebus: *ayo* 'metal, iron'. *sathiya* 'svastika glyph' Rebus: *sattva,* jasta 'zinc'.

It may be hypothesised that the altar worshipped by Tukulti-Ninurta I was also an altar like the Pyrennes altar used in bronze-age metallurgy. Further researches are needed to test this hypothesis. The 'rod' on the Tukulti-Ninurta altar may be rebus, as noted by Sigmund Freud commenting on the narrative shown on the altar, as a re-enactment of a dream. It could also be rebus for a Meluhha gloss remembered as a cultural memory. *koṭi* banner, flag, streamer (Tamil) Rebus: *koḍ* 'artisan's workplace'. Together with this rod, the ring held in Ishtar's or Shamash's hands may be rebus too: पेढी (Gujarati. Marathi). पेंढें 'rings' Rebus: पेढी 'shop' while recognizing their function as: *kaḍiyo, kaḍiyaṇa* 'divine architects'.

Apkallu, priest of Enki

Apkallu is shown in two ligatures: one with wings and one with fish (Contextual glyphs relate to tree and water). Masked as Enki, half-fish and half-priest; from a relief of Assurnasirpal II (883--859 BCE).

Grapheme: kōli = a stubble of jōḷa (Kannada) kōle a stub or stump of corn (Telugu) Rebus: kol 'working in iron' (cf. Ear of corn held in Apkallu's right hand). ayo 'fish' Rebus: ayo 'metal, iron'. kamaṭha 'pot' Rebus: kammaṭa 'portable furnace, crucible'. Mlekh 'goat' Rebus: milakkha 'copper'. eraka 'wing' Rebus: eraka 'copper'. [*kol, kolhe* '*koles* are a group of people who are iron smelters and speak a language akin to that of Santals.']

Assur smelting iron near Netrahat, not far from Malhar on Ganga basin which yielded an archaeological artifact of an iron smelter dated to ca. 18th century BCE. "Villagers reported (as a tradition) passed down from several generations, that the agarias (a particular tribe known for their smelting skills) from Robertsganj side, used to come in this area to procure iron by smelting the hematite' (Rakesh Tiwari)."[70]

Iron smelter ca. 1800 BCE Lohardewa, Malhar. Circular clay furnace comprising iron slag and tuyures and other waste materials stuck with its body, exposed at Lohsanwa mound, Period II, Malhar,, District Chandauli.[71]

•Glyphs: giant ear of corn, eagle wings, antelope, sacred pot, fish

•Source: Apkallu Angel, Fig. of Apkallu from Nimrud, ancient Mesopotamia (north-west palace, room Z, 875-860 BCE).[72]

Lishtar notes: "The apkallu were also known as the priests of Enki…Enki's organized world…in which wealth can be brought to the Land as a whole. " (Lishtar, 2000, *Understanding Enki and the world order*). kulullu, 'fish-man; kuliltu, 'fish-woman'; fish-garbed figure: apkallu, 'sage' (in fish-guise); from Calah. Gypsum. Height ca. 2.5 m.[73]

A few examples[74] of Ancient Mesopotamian Religious Iconography from different kudurru´s:

Kudurru of Gula-Eresh, showing a lamp (centre) as a symbol of Nuṣku (BM 102485). Nuṣka/Nuṣku (god) A god of fire and light, and minister of Enlil. Kudurru of Gula-Eresh, showing a lamp (centre) as a symbol of Nuṣku (BM 102485). Limestone kudurru or boundary

stone recording a gift of land; the symbols above the writing represent gods; two registers of divine symbols; Limestone kudurru or boundary stone: consisting of a boulder of dark limestone, the faces of which have been slightly flattened by rubbing in order to take inscriptions and sculptures in relief. The stone tapers rather more towards the top than towards the base. The upper portion of the Obverse, for a space of 9 1/4 in., and the right side and part of the left side of the stone, are engraved in low relief with a series of emblems, the greater number of which are arranged within two registers separated by plain bands. Faces A and B, Upper register, (1) Solar disc, (2) Crescent, (3) Eight-pointed star, (4) Horned headdress upon a shrine, (5) Horned headdress upon a shrine, (6) Turtle upon a shrine, (7) Twin spirals upon a shrine (the spirals here curl inward and spring from a stem, thus presenting striking differences from the so-called inverted yoke), (8) Wedge upon a shrine (the thicker end of the wedge is here indented, and its face is ornamented with a decorative band), and (9) Spear-head upon a shrine; Lower register, (10) Lightning-fork upon a shrine, (11) Lamp upon a shrine, (12) Yoke upon a shrine, (13) Scorpion upon a shrine, (14) Dog upon a shrine, (15) Lion-headed mace a upon a shrine; below the second register on Face B, (16) Sheaf of corn upon a shrine; Left side and top of stone, (17) Serpent. The emblems in the Lower register are separated from the shrines on which they rest by a plain band. Below twin spirals, wedge upon a shrine and spear upon a shrine in the Upper register the engraver has left a similar band, but there he has cut it into sections, each of which forms a base for an emblem or a heavy cornice for its shrine. The lower part of the Obverse and the whole of the Reverse are devoted to the text, which records a deed of a gift recording a grant of five 'gur' of corn-land, in the district of Edina in Southern Babylonia, to Gula-eresh by Eanna-shum-iddina, governor of the Sea-Land. The estate is described as bounded by Bit-Iddiatu, the estate of Amel-Marduk, the province of the Sea-Land, and the Edina-Canal. The surveyor was Amurru-bel-zeri, and the transfer was completed by Zakiru and Adad-shum-ibni, two high officials. [75]

ISHTAR
SIN
SHAMASH
ANU
ENLIL
EA
NINHURSAG
NERGAL
ZABABA
NINURTA
NABU
MARDUK
GULA
ADAD
SHALA
NUSHKU
divinités agraires cassites
NINGHIZZIDA
SHUMALIYA ?
ISHARA

An attempt has been made to read rebus in Meluhha some of the hieroglyphs on these artifacts.

Uruk.

Proto-elamite accounting tablet with tree and other Meluhha hieroglyphs

Administrative tablet with cylinder seal impression of a

male figure, hunting dogs, and boars, 3100–2900 B.C.; Jemdet Nasr period (Uruk III script) Mesopotamia Clay; H. 2 in. (5.3 cm) The seal impression depicts a male figure guiding two dogs on a leash and hunting or herding boars in a marsh environment. Traces of tree on platform are visible to the left of the jackal (?).

Ur cylinder seal with tabernae Montana plant, BM 122947. Tagar 'a flowering shrub, a plant in bloom'

(Gujarati); 'the shrub tabernae Montana coronaria, and a fragrant powder or perfume obtained from it, incense (Vin 1.203); tagara, 'fragrant wood' (Prakrit) Rebus: tagromi 'tin metal alloy' (Kuwi) tagaram 'tin' (Malayalam)

Cylinder-seal - the "priest-king" and his acolyte

feeding the sacred flock

<DaLO>(MP) {N} ``^branch, ^twig". *Kh.<DaoRa>(D) `dry leaves when fallen', ~<daura>, ~<dauRa> `twig', Sa.<DAr>, Mu.<Dar>, ~<Dara> `big branch of a tree', ~<DauRa> `a twig or small branch with fresh leaves on it', So.<kOn-da:ra:-n> `branch', H.<DalA>, B.<DalO>, O.<DaLO>, Pk.<DAlA>. %7811. #7741.(Munda etyma) Rebus: *ḍhālako* = a large metal ingot (G.) *ḍhālakī* = a metal heated and poured into a mould; a solid piece of metal; an ingot (Gujarati)

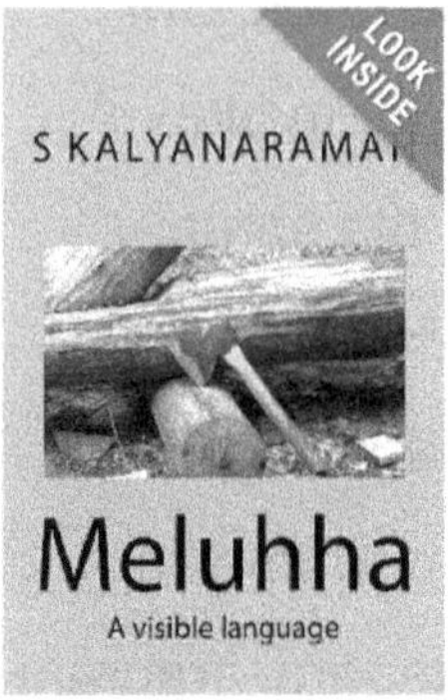

A number of rebus hieroglyphs have been indicated in the context of *Meluhha – A visible language.*[76]

tamar, 'palm tree, date palm' (Hebrew) Rebus reading would be: *tam(b)ra*, 'copper' (Prakrit)

kamaṭa 'spouted pot' Rebus: *kammaṭa* 'mint, coiner, portable gold furnace'.

khōṇḍa 'leafless tree' (Marathi). Rebus: *kõdār* 'turner' (Bengali)

khaṇḍa 'divisions', Rebus: *kāṇḍā* 'metalware'

kammaṭa 'crucible' Rebus: 'mint'

karaḍa 'safflower', *karaḍa* 'duck' Rebus: *karaḍa* 'hard alloy' *kalāda* 'goldsmith workshop'

dula 'pair' Rebus: *dul* 'cast metal'

āra 'serpent' Rebus: *āra* 'brass'

meḍ 'step' Rebus: meḍ 'iron'

Alternative: *aḍi* 'foot' Rebus: *aṭai, aḍi* அடை 'anvil'

uṭu 'arrowhead', Rebus: *uḍu* 'boat

kuṭi 'drink' Rebus: *kuṭhi* 'smelter'.

tagara 'antelope, ram' Rebus: *damgar* 'merchant'

meḍho a ram, a sheep Rebus: *mẽṛhẽt, meḍ* 'iron'

ḍangar 'bull' Rebus: *ḍangar* 'blacksmith' (Hindi)

pattar 'trough' Rebus: *pattar* 'smiths' guild'
uṭu 'Feather of an arrow; Arrow-head' Rebus: *uḍu* 'boat, raft'.
scorpion *bica* 'scorpion' (Assamese) Rebus: *bica* 'stone ore'. meṛed-bica 'iron stone ore'. *koṇḍi* the sting of a scorpion.).Rebus: *kõdā* 'to turn in a lathe' (Bengali) कोंद *kōnda* 'engraver, lapidary setting or infixing gems' (Marathi)
turtle or tortoise *kamaṭhamu*. [Skt.] n. A tortoise. Rebus: kammaṭa (Kannada) కమటము *kamaṭamu*. [Telugu] n. A portable furnace for melting the precious metals. అగసాలెవాని కుంపటి. (Telugu)
snake and snake-hood: *āra* 'serpent' Rebus: *āra* 'brass'. *paṭam* , *n.* < *phaṭa*. 'cobra's hood' (CDIAL 9040). Rebus: 'sharpness of iron': *padm* (obl.*padt-*) temper of iron (Kota)(DEDR 3907); *patam* 'sharpness, as of the edge of a knife' (Tamil)
duck *karaṇḍa* 'duck' (Sanskrit) *karaṛa* 'a very large aquatic bird' (Sindhi) Rebus: करडा [karaḍā] Hard from alloy--iron, silver &c. (Marathi)
fox *lōī* f., *lō* m.2. Pr. *ẓuwī* 'fox' (Western Pahari)(CDIAL 11140-2). Rebus: *loh* 'copper' (Hindi).

ram मेंढा [mēṇḍhā] *m* (मेष S through H) A male sheep, a ram or tup.(Marathi) *meḍ* 'iron' (Mundari. Remo.)
Frog hieroglyph: *meḍak* 'small frog' (Gujarati) Rebus: *meḍ* 'iron' (Ho.)

mũh 'face'; rebus: metal ingot (Santali) mũhā = the quantity of iron produced at one time in a native smelting furnace of the Kolhes; iron produced by the Kolhes and formed like a four-cornered piece a little pointed at each end; mūhā mẽṛhẽt = iron smelted by the Kolhes and formed into an equilateral lump a little pointed at each end; kolhe tehen me~ṛhe~t mūhā akata = the Kolhes have to-day produced pig iron (Santali)

Footstep hieroglyph: Rebus 1: Ta. aṭi foot, footprint, base, bottom, source, origin; Ma. aṭi sole of foot, footstep, measure of foot, Ko. aṛy foot (measure);To. oṛy foot. Ka. aḍi foot, measure of foot, step, pace,Te. aḍugu foot, footstep, footprint, step, pace, measure of a foot,aḍi-ga_r_ra sandal, wooden shoe. Ga. (S.2) aḍugu footstep (< Te.). Go. (G.) aḍi beneath;

(Mu.)(DEDR 72) Rebus 2: Glyph: *Ko.* meṭ- (mec-) to trample on, tread on; meṭ sole of foot, footstep, footprint. Rebus: *meḍ* 'iron' (Mundari. Remo.) Lizard hieroglyph: Glyph: araṇe 'lizard' (Tulu) Rebus: eraṇi f. ' anvil ' (Gujarati); aheraṇ, ahiraṇ, airaṇ, airṇī, haraṇ f. (Marathi)

"…a number of cases have been shown where the Prakrits retain forms which are more archaic than the equivalents in the earliest Vedic, showing that these dialects, known from early inscriptions (such as those of King Ashoka in the mid-third century BCE), from the early writings of Buddhists and Jainas, and from the early Sanskrit dramas, were contemporary with the Sanskrit of that period. For the earlier Vedic period, though there is no direct evidence for any form of speech other than Vedic, the coexistence of contemporaneous 'prakritic' varieties must be inferred. Cf . Emeneau's comment: 'We have an inkling…of the oldest Indo-Aryan of North India as a large dialect area whose speakers were unified by a common culture and by the religion that provides us with the evidential documents; there probably were other dialects as well, outside of this social and religious milieu...' Regarding the question of a Prakrit contemporary with the Rigveda, Emeneau notes: 'Tedesco...prefers to call this dialect parallel to Rgvedic 'archaic Middle Indic'; probably 'Proto-Middle-Indo-Aryan (or Indic)' is as good. No absolute chronology is possible for it...But we can guess that the latter [Proto-Middle Indo-Aryan] type of dialect was in existence from the beginning of the time-span.' Diglossia. That this was a diglossic relationship, and not simply dialectical variation, is shown by the existence from early times of 'hyper-Sanskritized' forms, that is, Vedic or Sanskrit forms which were treated as if they were Prakrit, ad 'sanskritized' to avoid the appearance that the speaker/writer was using a Prakrit form." (pp.53-54) (Southworth, Franklin C., 2005, *Linguistic Archaeology of South Asia*, Routledge Curzon).

"It is now generally agreed by most authorities on the subject that the Aryan linguistic vestiges in the Near East are to be connected specifically with Indo-Aryan, and not with Iranian, and also that they do not represent a third, independent Aryan group, and are not to be ascribed to the hypothetically reconstructed Proto-Aryan." (Burrow, T., 1973, The Proto-Indiaryans, *Journal of the Royal Asiatic Society of Great Britain and Ireland*, No. 2(1973), pp. 123-140.) The Kayanians were smiths. Avestan hero, Keresaaspa (of manly mind, valiant, *naire.manah*) lived later than Aathwyas. Arthur Christensen in his *Les Kayanides* deals with eight Kavi-s in the ancient history of Iran. (Christensen, Arthur, 1931, *Les Kayanides*, Kobenhavn, Andr. Fred. Host & son, (French), pp. 99-104).

Pomegranates lined up on altars. Request for provenience information has been sought for this remarkable artifact which is perhaps from Ancient Near East.[77]

Hormuz

"Today, Hormuz survives as the name of a historic island in the Iranian province of Hormozgan…Every Zoroastrian knows that Hormuz or Hormozd is also a Middle Persian word or term for God in Zoroastrianism. Hormozd itself is the derivative of the original Avestan/Old Iranian term Ahura Mazda via an intermediate derivative, Ahurmazd (transition between Old and Middle Persian)…Moroccan traveller Ibn Battuta (1304-c. 1368) wrote in his travelogue, 'I travelled next to the country of Hormuz. Hormuz is a town on the coast, also called Mughistan.' Ibn Battuta's Mughistan (Moghistan) was an alternative name for the country of Hormuz, today's Hormozgan. It is a name that continued to be used on European maps in the 18th and 19th century.

Mughistan/Moghistan by definition means the land of the Mugh/Mogh. Mugh (derived from magha), means a Zoroastrian priest – nown to the West as a magus. The plural is mughan as in pir-e mughan/moghan, the hoary and wise magi…Hormozgan was a junction point of ancient land and sea…Zoroastrian era trade—c. 3000 BCE to 650 CE. The strategic position of the archaeological sites found in the Old Hormuz-Minab region, combined with the archaeological evidence of early contact by sea with India, suggests that the region and Kingdom of Hormuz, was already actively involved in long-distance trade by the 1st millennium BCE. Parallels with Tepe Yahya in particular, up the Persian Gulf (c. 326 BCE?), there was clearly a substantial enough settled coastal population to have left some impression in the Green sources. The presence of the Red Polished Ware from the Indian sub-continent suggests that Hormuz was as important to Indian trade in the Zoroastrian era as it was in the more recent historic past…Painted black-on-orange wares characteristic of period IVC at

Tepe Yahya (c 3100-2900 BCE) was found at one prehistoric site, K 14."

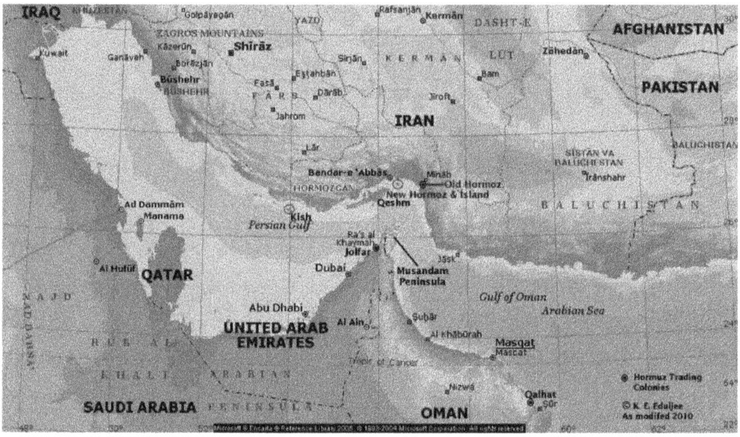

"The earliest site (K 9) recorded thus far yielded sherds comparable to so-called "Lapui" ware, of early fourth-millennium date, from sites like Tal-e Bākun in the Marvdašt, Fārs province (Prickett, 1986, p. 1270). Most of the prehistoric sites[78] recorded, however, have been dated on the basis of parallels to Tepe Yaḥyā in east-central Kermān province. A single prehistoric site (K 14) was characterized by painted black-on-orange wares paralleled in period IVC at Tepe Yaḥyā (ca. 3100-2900 B.C.E.), but the greatest number of prehistoric sites in the area show parallels to the Iron Age and Parthian-period levels there (e.g., K 84, 96, 98, 100, 104-6, 109, 110B, 112, 124-26, 130G, 137)... the strategic position of the archeological sites found in the Minab region, combined with the archeological evidence of contact by sea with India, suggests that the region, which later became so important under the Kingdom of Hormuz, was already actively involved in long-distance trade by the 1st millennium B.C.E. Parallels with Tepe Yaḥyā, in particular, suggest that we may, however, push back the threshold of inter-regional involvement into the 3rd millennium B.C.E...The presence of Indian Red Polished Ware suggests that the Straits of Hormuz were as important to Indian Ocean trade in the late pre-Islamic era as they were in the more recent historic past. "[79]

"From the 3rd millennium BC onwards Mesopotamian cuneiform sources mention fruits (Sumerian nig-sa-(h)a, Akkadian (a)zamru or muthummu) and fruit cultivation (Postgate 1987; Powell 1987; Joannes 2001). While some species are well identified, such as date (Sum. zu-lum; Aide, suluppu), grape (Sum. gestin; Aide, kardnu), fig (Sum. pes; Aide, tittu), and pomegranate (Sum. nu-ur-ma; Aide, nurmu), in other cases it is difficult to match a Sumerian or Akkadian name with a particular botanical species. Fruit appear in lexical lists, records of economic transactions, notes of delivery to temples and palaces, legal documents, medical texts, descriptions of banquets, and lists of offerings to deities."[80]

The architectural monument of Shalmaneser III (c. 858-824 BCE), ekal masharti (Fort Shalmaneser) occupied the southeast corner of the city enclosure at Nimrud. Upper parts of walls are decorated with rows of impressed rosettes in glazed brick. "...throne room...In the lower entre panel two kings stand facing one another below a winged disk containing 'Assur', then comes the inscription, and above it rampant bulls, heads turned back, flanking a tree. The whole design is framed first by rossettes and guilloches, then by a triple border; from inside to out, of alternating pomegranates and buds; of kneeling goats and palmettes. The glaze colours were green, yellow, white and black on an entirely (originally ultramarine) blue

background."[81] It is the palace of Ashur-nasirpal II.

Austen Henry Layard's rendering the Throne Room in the Northwest Palace.[82]

Meluhha glosses

मेढ [mēḍha] The polar star (Marathi). [cf.The eight-pointed star associated with the feminine divinity in Mesopotamian tradition.] Glyph of the implement she carries on her left hand: *koṭṭï katti* billhook (Koḍagu) Horned diadem: kirīṭa n. ' diadem, crest ' Rebus: kirāṭa m. ' merchant '; *koḍ* horn' *Rebus: koḍ* 'workshop'.

karamarda m. ' the tree Carissa carandas ' MBh., *°aka* -- m. ' the tree ', n. ' its fruit ' Suśr., *°mardī* -- f. lex. 2. *karamārja -- . [Cf. kāsamarda -- ~ *kāsamārja --]1. Pa. *karamadda* -- , *°manda* -- m., Pk. *karamadda* -- , *°maṁda* -- m., *°vaṁdī* -- f.; S. *karno* m. ' a tree with a sweet -- smelling white flower '; P. *karaũdā* m. ' Carissa carandas ', B. *karaṇḍā*, Or. *karandā*, Mth. *karonā*, H. *karaũdā*, G. *karamdī* f. ' the tree ', *°dũ* n. ' the fruit ', M. *karvãd*, *°dī* f. ' the tree ', *°vãd*, *°vãdũ* n. ' the fruit', *karãdā*, *°rãdā*, *°rĩdā*, *kārãdā* m., *karãd* f. ' the tree ', n. ' the fruit ', Si. *karam̃ba* (< **karambda* <

**karamaňda*?).2. N. *karaũji* ' a partic. kind of acid fruit used for making pickles '. (CDIAL 2799).

kirīṭa1 n. ' diadem, crest ' MBh., *tirīṭa* -- 1 n. lex. [Similar alternance of *k* -- and *t* -- in kirīṭi -- ~ tirīṭa -- 2]Pa. *kirīṭa* -- n.m.; Pk. *kirīḍa* -- ' diadem ', *tirīḍa* -- m.n. ' headdress '; Si. *kiruḷa* ' crown '. (CDIAL 3176).

kirāṭa m. ' merchant ' Rājat., *kirīṭa* -- 2 m. BhP., *kírāta*-- m. ' a degraded mountain tribe ' VS., *cilātī* -- f. ' woman of this tribe ' YogH. [Alternance of *k* -- and *c* -- , -- *ṭ* -- and -- *t*<-> suggests Drav. origin, EWA i 211. Perh. same as kilāta -- ' dwarf '] Pa. *kirāṭa* -- m. ' fraudulent merchant ' (*kirāṭa* -- , *°āta*<-> m. ' man of a jungle tribe ' see *kilāta* --); Pk. *kirāḍa* -- , *°āya* -- , *cilāa* -- m., f. *°āī* -- , *°āiyā* -- ' a non -- Aryan tribe, slave ', *cilāī* -- f.; S. *kirāṛu* m. ' Hindu shopkeeper '; L. *kirāṛ*, *karāṛ* m., *kirāṛī* f. ' member of a tribe of Hindus (also called *aroṛā*) who act as traders and moneylenders '; H. *kirāṛ* m. ' merchant '. -- Deriv. Pa. *kērāṭika* -- , *°iya*<-> ' false ' (cf. *kirāsa* -- ' fraudulent '); -- L. *kirṛakkā* ' connected with Hindus '.(CDIAL 3173).

kirīṭī f. ' Andropogon aciculatus ', *kiriṭi* -- n. ' fruit of the marshy date palm (Phoenix paludosa) '. [Cf. tirīṭa -- 2 and similar alternance of initial in kirīṭa -- 1 and tirīṭa -- 1]S. *kiriṛī* f. ' a tree growing in salt marshes (Ceriops canolleana) '. (CDIAL 3177).

hintāla m. ' the marshy date -- palm Phoenix paludosa ' Hariv. [Cf. tāḍa -- 3] Pa. *hintāla* -- m. ' Phoenix paludosa ', B. *hĩtāl, hẽt°*; Si. *hitul* ' the swamp date – 'palm ', *kitul* (X *kaduru* < kharjū´ra -- ?).(CDIAL 14093).

*sippī ' shell '. [← Drav. Tam. *cippi* DED 2089] Pa. *sippī* -- , *sippikā* -- f. ' pearl oyster ', Pk. *sippī* -- f., S. *sipa* f.; L. *sipp* ' shell ', *sippī* f. ' shell, spathe of date palm ', (Ju.) *sip* m., *sippī* f. ' bivalve shell '; P. *sipp* m., *sippī* f. ' shell, conch '; Ku. *sīp, sīpi* ' shell '; N. *sipi* ' shell, snail shell '; B. *sip* ' libation pot ', *chip* ' a kind of swift canoe ' S. K. Chatterji CR 1936, 290 (or < kṣiprá -- ?); Or. *sipa* ' oyster shell, mother -- of -- pearl, shells burnt for lime '; Bi. *sīpī* ' mussel shells for lime '; OAw. *sīpa* f. ' bivalve shell ', H. *sīp* f.; G. *sīp* f. '

half an oyster shell ', *chīp* f. ' shell '; M. *śīp*, *śīp* f. ' a half shell ', *śīpā* m. ' oyster shell '; -- Si.*sippiya* ' oyster shell ' ← Tam. (CDIAL 13417).

*sindī ' date -- palm '.Pk. *siṁdī*, *siṁdōlī* -- f. ' date -- palm '; M. *śĩd*, *śĩdī*, *śĩdhī* f. ' wild date -- palm '. (CDIAL 13410).

sindūra1 n. (*sindūrikā* -- f. lex.) ' red lead, vermilion ' Kathās. 2. saindūra -- ' coloured with red lead ' Ratnāv.1. Pk. *siṁdūra* -- n. ' red lead ', K. *sẹndürü* f., S. *sinduru* m., P. *sā̃dhūr* m., Ku.gng. *sinūr*, N. *sĩdur*, *sĩdhur*, *sinur*, A. *xindur*, B. *sĩdur*, Or.*sĩdūra*, Mth. *sindur*, H. *sindūr* m. (*sindūrā* m. ' box of red lead '), G. *sindūr*, Ko. *śindūru.*
2. Pk. *seṁdūra* -- n. ' red lead ', A. *xendur* (*xenduri* ' red as vermilion '), Bi. Mth. *sẽdur*, *senur*, Bhoj. *senur*, H. *sẽdūr* m.; M. *śẽdūr* m. ' red lead ', *śẽdrā* ' coloured with it '. WPah.kṭg. *səndūr* m. ' red pigment (vermilion) ' prob. ← H. Him.I 218, Garh. *sindūr.* (CDIAL 13411).

*satkharjūra ' cultivated date -- palm '. [sánt -- , kharjū´ra --] Si. *sakaduru* ' date -- palm, Phoenix zelanica '? (CDIAL 13110).

śā´khā f. ' branch ' RV. Pa. *sākhā* -- f., *°kha* -- n. ' branch ', Pk. *sāhā* -- f.; Ash. *ċau*, *sau* ' branch, ear of corn '; Wg. *ċāw*, *ċōw* ' branch ', Kt. *ċåw* f., Pr. *ċāw*; WPah.jaun. *śā̃h* ' bough '; Or. *sāhā* ' branch, crossbars between shafts of bullock carts ', *sāhi* ' line, row, row of neighbouring houses '; Si. *sā* ' branch '; -- ext. -- *l* -- : Pk. *sāhulī* -- , *°liā* -- f. ' branch '; Ku. *saũlā* pl. ' green shoots or twigs '; N. *syāulo* ' a cut branch '; M. *sāũḷ* f.n., *sāvḷī* f. ' branch of various trees (palm, coconut, betel) '.

śākhyá -- ; śākhāmr̥ga -- ; víśākhā -- ; karaśākhā -- , *dvāraśākhī -- WPah.kṭg. *śā̃* f. (*śaĩ*) ' branch ', jaun. *śā̃h.* (CDIAL 12376).

śākhyá ' belonging to or resembling a branch, branching ' Pāṇ. [śā´khā --] Phal. *šāk*, *šākhā* (pl.?) ' wood, tree '. (CDIAL 12379).

bhramara1 ' *moving unsteadily, revolving ' (m. ' potter's wheel ' lex.), *bhramaraka* -- m. ' spinning top '

Bālar., ' whirlpool, lock of hair ' lex. [Cf. *bhramá* -- m. ' flame ' RV. -- √bhram] Pa. *bhamarikā* -- f. ' humming top '; Pk. *bhamarī* -- , *bhamalī* -- , *°liyā* -- f. ' dizziness '; K. *bambur* m. ' flurry '; S. *bhaũrī* f. ' curl '; L. *bhãvar* m. ' whirlpool ', *bhãvarī* f. ' whirl of date -- palm leaves '; P. *bhãvar* f. ' whirlpool ', *bhaũrī*, *bhaurī* f. ' curl of hair '; Ku. *bhaũr*, *bhaũro* m., *bhaũrī* f. ' whirlpool, whirlwind, tempest '; N. *bhũwari*, *bhumari*, *bhaũri* ' whirlwind, whirl, whorl of hair, crown of head '; Or. *bhaũra* ' turning lathe ', *bhaãra* ' auger, gimlet ', *bhaũrā*, *bhaĩrā* ' spinning top ', *pāṇibhaũri* ' whirlpool '; Bi. *bhaũr -- kalī* ' iron link fastened to rope close to oilmill bullock's neck ', *bhaũriyā* ' ploughing a field round and round '; OAw. *bhaṁvara* m. ' whirlpool '; H. *bhãwar*, *bhaũr*, *bhaur* m. ' whirlpool ', *bhaũrī* f. ' revolution, lock of hair '; G. *bhamar* f. ' whirlpool ', *bhamrɔ* m. ' large do. ', *bhamrī* f. ' giddiness ', *bhamarṛɔ* m. ' spinning top '; M. *bhõvrā* m. ' whorl of hair ', *bhõvrī* f. ' whirling round '; Ko. *bhõvro* ' spinning top '; Si. *bamaraya*, *bamarē*, *baṁbaraya* ' humming top ', *baṁburu* ' curled ', *baṁburu -- kes* ' curl '; -- prob. Paš.ar. *blämúr*, kuṛ. *lāmbəl -- bṛak* ' lightning ', Gaw. Sv. *lāmaċúlik* (IIFL iii 3, 110 < **bhramala* --

).bhrāmarī -- .Md. *bumaru* ' spinning top '. (CDIAL 9650).

10146 mukula n. ' bud ' Suśr., *makula* -- 2 n. lex. 2. mukura -- , *makura* -- 2 n. lex. 3. *bakula -- 2. [Cf. similar interchange of initial in bakula -- 1. -- ← Drav., Tam. *mokkuḷ* &c., DED 4007; also *mudgara* -- 2 m. ' bud ' lex. with same variation of -- *k* -- ~ -- *dg* -- as in mukuṣṭha--] 1. Pa. *makula* -- m. ' bud ', Pk. *maüla* -- m.n.; S. *mora* f. ' budding ', *moṛro* m. ' fresh new leaf '. 2. Pk. *maüra* -- m.n. ' bud '; H. *maur* m. ' bud, blossom '; G. *mɔhɔr* m. ' blossom '.3. MB. *baula*, B. *bol* ' bud, blossom of fruit tree, knob of a wooden clog '; Or. *baüḷa* ' mango bud '; Aw.lakh. *baur* ' mango blossom '. (CDIAL 10146).

mukulayati ' *blossoms '. 2. mukurayati. 3. mukulāyatē. [*mukulayati* (tr.), *°lāyatē* (intr.) ' closes (like a bud) ' Kāv., *°litá* -- R., *°lāyita*-- Kāv. ' having blossoms ', *mukurita* -- ' id.? ' Pāṇ.gaṇa. -- mukula --]1. Pk. *maülēi* ' blossoms '; S. *morjaṇu* ' to sprout '; P. *maulnā* ' to blossom, bud '; Ku. *maulṇo* ' to flourish ', N. *maulanu*, B. *maulā* ' to

blossom ', H. *maulnā.* 2. H. *maurnā* ' to blossom ', G. *mɔrvũ.*3. Pk. *maülāaï* ' blossoms ', N. *maulāunu,* H. *maulānā.* (CDIAL 10147).
Ta. tār flower, blossom, flower-bud. *Ma.* tār flower, bud, lotus. (DEDR 3165).

Ta. taḷir (-pp-, -tt-) to shoot forth, sprout, put forth leaves, flourish, prosper, rejoice; *n.* sprout, tender shoot; taḷirppu sprouting. *Ma.* taḷir bud, new leaf, shoot; taḷirkka to bud, sprout, get fresh leaves; taḷirppu, taḷirmma budding. *Ko.* tayḷ breed of cattle. *Ka.* taḷal to bud, sprout, shoot; taḷito shoot, sprout, put forth leaves; *n.* race, family, stock, breed; taḷir to shoot, sprout, put forth leaves; *n.* young shoot, sprout, new leaf or new leaves. *Tu.* taḷirů sprout, bud. *Te.* talaru to bloom, shine, thrive; taliru a sprout, shoot; talirucu to sprout, shoot, bloom. *Kuwi* (Isr.) dāl- (-it-) to blossom. (DEDR 3131).

Ta. tuḷir- (-pp-, -tt-) to bud, sprout, shoot, put forth leaves, prosper, thrive; *n.* bud, sprout, young leaf, tender foliage. *Ma.* tuḷir a bud; tuḷirkkato bud. *Ka.* suṟi tender sprout; (Bark.) suḷi, (Hal.)

culi sprout; (Rabakavi, *LSB* 5.19) tɔḷəlu mango shoot. *Koḍ.* cuḷi leaf shoot. *Tu.* suḷi a tender shoot, germ or bud. *Malt.* cúle to sprout; cúlo blade of grass or corn.(CDIAL 3362).

tū´la1 n. ' tuft of grass or reeds, panicle of flower or plant ' AV., ' cotton ' MBh., ' pencil ' Divyāv., m. ' cotton ' lex., *tūlaka* -- n. ' cotton ', *tūlā* -- , *°lī* -- f. ' cotton, wick ' lex., *tū´li* -- f. ' painter's brush ', *°likā* -- f. ' panicle used as probing rod, wick ' lex., *tūda* -- 1 m. ' the cotton tree ' lex. [Poss. ← Drav. Tam. *tūral* ' painter's brush, shoot ' DED 2790. -- Cf. turī --]Pa. *tūla* -- n. ' tuft of grass, cotton ', *tūlikā* -- f. ' mattress (of layers of grass or wool) '; Pk. *tūla* -- n. ' cotton -- wool ', *tūlī* -- f. ' paint -- brush ',*tūliā* -- f. ' mattress stuffed with cotton, paint -- brush '; Ḍ. *tūli* f. ' kettledrum -- stick '; Paš. *tuléč* ' thread ' (< **tūlikyā* -- ?), *tulča* ' spindle '; Kho. (Lor.) *tuli dik* ' to cast lots (by means of sticks) ', *tuleini* ' pin with which antimony is applied to eyes '; Sh. (Lor.) *tūli* ' little stick or splinter (e.g. that used for threading string through waistband) ', *tulu* ' iron spindle on which bobbin is placed '; K. *tūl* m. ' cotton wool ', *tal*, *tul* f. ' needle, stylus for applying collyrium to eyes, painter's brush ', *tulu* m. ' single blade of grass or straw ', *tujü, tàji, tüjü, tülü* f. ' small stick (such as a straw or hair of a brush) '; S. *tūru* m. ' crop of such plants as spring up for a second or third time ', *tūli* f. ' mattress, bedding ' (← L.); L. *tūl* f. ' underbedding of nuptial couch '; A. *tulā* ' ginned cotton ', *tuli* ' mattress, painter's brush '; B. *tulā, tolā* ' cotton ', *tuli* ' wick, painter's brush '; Or. *tuḷā* ' picked cotton ', *tuḷi* ' cotton, quilt stuffed with cotton, painter's brush '; Bi. *tūr* ' cleaned cotton '; Mth. *tū̆r* cotton -- wool '; G. *tūr* n. ' tree -- cotton ', *tūḷ*n. ' young corn plants ' (< **tulla* --); Si. *tili* ' mattress '.tūla -- 2 ' mulberry ' see tūta -- . tūla -- 3 ' a musical instrument ' see tūra -- .S.kcch. *tūr* m. ' cotton of the *āṅkḍo* tree '; WPah.kṭg. *tvḷi* f. ' tuft of grass '.(CDIAL 5904).

Ta. malar (-v-, -nt-) to open as a flower, bloom, be expanded, extended or spread, be cheerful, beam with joy, be wide open as a gate, (*lex.*) appear, rise to view; (-pp-, -tt-) to cause to flower; *n.* full-blown flower, blossom; malarcci blossoming, blooming, freshness, cheerfulness; malarttu (malartti-) to cause to flower, open out (as closed hand or umbrella); malarppu causing to blossom, exposing (as one's chest); malarōṉ Brahmā, as seated on a lotus. *Ma.* malar full-blown flower; malaruka to open as a flower, be fried as grain, be concave, corolla-like; *tr.* malarttuka; malarccaexpanding. *Ka.* malar, maral flower. *Te.* (K.) malãcu to flower, blossom. ? *Br.* maling to open, undo, untie; malinging to be opened, undone, untied, begin (rain), get up (wind).(DEDR 4739).

páttra n. ' wing -- feather ' VS., ' wing ' (in cmpd.) RV., ' leaf, petal ' KātyŚr., ' leaf of book ' Kāv., *°traka* -- m.n. lex., *°trikā* -- f. Kāv. [< earlier *pátra* -- Wackernagel AiGr ii 2, 855. -- See also paṭṭa -- 1. -- √pat] Pa. *patta* -- n. ' wing, feather, leaf ', *°tī* -- , *°tikā* -- f. ' leaf '; Pk. *patta* -- , *°taya* -- n., *°tiā* -- f. ' wing, leaf, page '; Gy. eur. *patri, patrin* f. ' leaf '; Paš. *šāpātr* ' butterfly ' (← Orm. *šāparak* X **patr* < *páttra* -- IIFL iii 3, 165); Bshk. *pal* ' leaf ', Tor. *pāṣ*, K. *paṭhar*, dat. *°tras* m. (in cmpd.*dupotru* ' two -- leaved '); S. *paṭru* m. ' band of iron to tighten anything, tire of a wheel ', *chilu -- paṭru* m. ' goods and chattels ' (< '

*skin and feathers '?); L. *pattar* m. ' leaf, foliage ', *pattrā* m. ' palm -- leaf fibre ', (Ju.) *patrā* m. ' page ', *patrī* f. ' leaf ', awāṇ. *pattar*, pl. *patrā* m. ' leaf '; P.*patt*, *pattrā*, *pattā* m. ' leaf ', *pattrī*, *pattī* f. ' leaf, almanac, thin slip of iron '; WPah.bhal. *paṭḷ* n. ' leaf, ' bhiḍ. *paṭḷõ* n.; Ku. *pāt* ' leaf, leaves and grass ', *pāto* ' horoscope, metal plate used to repair something broken ', *pātī* ' leaves, letter '; N. *pāt* ' leaf ', *pāto* ' page, blade of a knife ', *pāti* ' leaf, flowers used in worship '; A. *pāt* ' leaf, page ', *patā* ' thin metal plate '; B. *pāt* ' leaf ', *pātā* ' leaf, blade ', *pāti* ' epistle '; Or. *pāta* ' metal -- foil ', *patā* ' eyelid ', *pātiā* ' thin slip of metal '; Bi. *pāt* ' leaf ', *pātā* ' blade of paddle ', *pātā*, *pattā* ' leaf of yoke of plough ' (semant. cf. pallava -- 1); Mth. *pāt*, *pattā* ' leaf, page, epistle '; Bhoj. *pāt*, *pataī* ' leaf ', Aw.lakh. *pātā*, *pātī*, H. *pāt* m. ' leaf, thin metal plate ', *pātā*, *pattā* m. ' leaf ', *pātī*,*pattī* f. ' leaf, epistle, clue '; G. *pātrũ*, *pātũ* n. ' leaf ', *pātrī* f. ' packet of leaves and flowers ', *pātī* f. ' epistle '; M. *pāt* n. ' eyelid, blade of tool or weapon ', m. ' pinnateshaped leaf ', *pātẽ* n. ' leaf, blade ', *pātī* f. ' narrow leaf '; Si. *pata* (pl. *pat*) ' wing, feather, leaf ', *patta* (pl. *patu* < *pattraka* --) ' board, stick

', *petta* (pl. *peti*) ' slice, thin piece of wood ', *pätta* ' slice, side of body, side ' (both < *pattrikā* --); Md. *fat*, *fai*, ' leaf '. -- Kaf. and Dard. forms with -- *ṭṭ* -- (cf. paṭṭa -- 1): Wg. *påṭ*, *pɔ̄ṭ*, *paṭā´* ' leaf '; Pr. *pəṭegē* ' feather ', *wəṭ* ' wing ', *wəṭëgë* ' letter paper '; Dm. *ph**lṭ ' leaf ', Paš.lauṛ. *paṭā*, gul. *pūṭ*, ar. *páḍḍak*, kuṛ. *phāṭak*, Shum. *páṭṭa* m., Woṭ. *paṛ* f., Gaw. *phaṭa*, Sh.gil. *păṭu̯* m. ' a long leaf ' (→ Ḍ. *poṭ*, pl. *p**lṭa m.), gur. *pāṭŭ* m. ' leaf ', jij. *p*lṭu, koh. păṭhu̯ m., pales. páṭhə.* (CDIAL 7733).

*tāḍa3 ' fan -- palm ', *tāḍī* -- 2 f. in *tāḍī* -- *puṭa* -- ' palm -- leaf ' Kād., *tāla* -- 2 m. ' Borassus flabelliformis ' Mn., *tālī* -- , *°lakī* -- f. ' palm -- wine ' W. [Cf. hintāla --]Pa. *tāla* -- m. ' fan -- palm ', Pk. *tāḍa* -- , *tāla* -- , *tala* -- m., *tāḍī* -- , *tālī* -- f., K. *tāl* m., P. *tāṛ* m., N. *tār* (*tāṛ* ← H.), A. *tāl*, B. *tāṛ*, Or. *tāṛa*,*tāṛi*, *tāḷa*, Bi. *tār*, *tāṛ*, OAw. *tāra*, H. G. *tāṛ* m., M. *tāḍ* m., Si. *tala.* -- Gy. gr. *taró* m., *tarí* f. ' rum ', rum. *tari* ' brandy ', pal. *tar* ' date -- spirit '; S. *tāṛī* f. ' juice of the palmyra '; P. *tāṛī* ' the fermented juice '; N. *tāṛī* ' id., yeast ' (← H.); A. *tāri* ' the fermented juice ', B. Or. *tāṛi*, Bi. *tārī*, *tāṛī*, Bhoj. *tāṛī*, H. *tāṛī* f. ' the juice, the fermented juice ';

G. *tāṛī* f. ' the juice ', M. *tāḍī* f. <-> X hintāla -- q.v. S.kcch. *tāṛ* m. ' palm tree '. 5752a †*tāḍarukṣa -- ' palmyra palm '. [tāḍa -- 3, rukṣá --]Md. *tāruk* ' palmyra '. (CDIAL 5750).

tāṭaṅka n. m. ' ear -- ornament (large ring ac. Apte) ' Pra- sannar., *tāḍaṅka* -- n. Rājat., *tālaṅka* -- m. Apte. [Cf. *tāḍīdala* -- n. ' ear -- ornament ' Kālid., *tāḍapattra* -- (= *tāḍaṅka* --) lex., *tālapattra* -- n. ' palm -- leaf, ear -- ornament ' (' gold cylinder ' ac. Apte) Kād.;*tālāṅka* -- ' palm leaf ' W.; *tāḍī* -- , *tālī* -- f. ' ornament ' lex. (← Drav. Tam. *tāli* ' neck ornament ', etc. DED 2594, EWA i 499), *tālaka* -- n. ' ornament ' ("shaped like palm leaf") BHSk. Association with, rather than derivation from, *tāḍa -- 3]H. *tāṛā̃k*, *°rā̃g* m. ' an ornament for the ear ', H. *tarkī* f. ' a kind of earring (made orig. from palm -- leaf ac. Platts UD) ' (CDIAL 5747).

kharjū´ra m. ' the date -- palm Phoenix sylvestris ' TS., n. ' its fruit ' Kathās., *°rī* -- f. ' the tree ' VarBr̥S., *°jura* -- m. lex., *°juraka* -- n. ' its fruit ' BHSk. 2. kharju -- 2 f. ' wild date tree ' lex.1. Pa. *khajjūrī* -- f. '

wild date -- palm '; Pk. *khajjūra* -- m., *°rī* -- f. ' date -- palm ', *°ra* -- n. ' its fruit '; K. *khaẓar*, *khüzür* m. ' its fruit '; S.*khajūri* f. ' the tree ' (*/*?); L. P. *khajūr* f. ' the tree and its fruit ', P. *khā̃jūr* f., Ku. *khā̃jūr*, N. *khajur*, A. *khāzur*, B. *khājur*, *khej°*; Or. *khajuri* ' the tree ', *khajurā* ' its fruit '; Bhoj. *khajūr* ' the tree ', H. *khajūr* m. f. ' tree and fruit ', *°riyā* f. ' a small variety and its fruit '; G. *khajurī* f. ' the tree ', *khajur* n. ' its fruit ', M. *khā̃jurī* f., *khā̃jūr* m.; Si. *kaduru* ' the tree ', mald. *kaduru* ' its fruit '. -- X hintāla -- q.v.

2. Pk. *khajja* -- m. ' a partic. tree '; S. *khajī* f. ' the datepalm Phoenix dactylifera ', L. P. *khajjī* f. ' date -- palm '. Md. *kaduru* ' dates '; A. also *khezur* AFD 136.

kharjūraka 3829 kharjūraka m. ' scorpion ' Vasantar. N. *khajuro* ' centipede ', Or. *khajriā*, H. *khajūrā* m. -- Poss. conn. H. *khajūrā* ' twisted '; M. *khā̃jurā* ' twisted (of thread) '.WPah.poet. *khəjuri* f.pl. ' small plaits (in hair of head) '.(CDIAL 3828).

Ta. katir (-pp-, -tt-) to shine, glow, become manifest, abound, increase; *n.* ray of light, beam, light; katirppu radiance; katiravaṉ sun. *Ma.*katir ray; ka tiram beauty, radiance; katiravan sun; katirkka to shoot rays or looks, be radiant; katirmma shining, beaming. *Ka.* kadir ray of light, splendour; kadaru, kaduru lustre. *Te.* kaduru to be produced, increase, spread. (DEDR 1193).

Ta. katir ear of grain, spear of grass. *Ma.* katir ear, spike of corn; katirkka to shoot into ears; katirppu a sprout, shoot. *Ka.* kadir spike of corn, ear. *Koḍ.* kadï ear (of paddy, wheat, etc.). *Tu.* kadirů ear of corn; kadpu ear of ripened corn. (DEDR 1194).

Tu. kandůka, kandaka ditch, trench. *Te.* kandakamu id. *Konḍa* kanda trench made as a fireplace during weddings. *Pe.* kanda fire trench. *Kui* kanda small trench for fireplace. *Malt.* kandri a pit. (DEDR 1214).

Ta. katir spinner's spindle. *Ma.* katir id. *Ka.* kadir, kadaru, kaduru id. *Tu.* kadůrů, kadirů, kadrů id. *Te.* kaduru id. *Ga.* (S.3) kadur an instrument used to spin threads from cotton. (DEDR 1195).

ḍāla1 m. ' branch ' Śīl. 2. *ṭhāla -- . 3. *ḍāḍha -- . [Poss. same as *dāla -- 1 and dāra -- 1: √dal, √d&rcirclemacr;. But variation of form supports PMWS 64 ← Mu.]1. Pk. *ḍāla* -- n. ' branch '; S. *ḍāru* m. ' large branch ', *ḍārī* f. ' branch '; P. *ḍāl* m. ' branch ', *°lā* m. ' large do. ', *°lī* f. ' twig '; WPah. bhal. *ḍā* m. ' branch '; Ku. *ḍālo* m. ' tree '; N. *ḍālo* ' branch ', A. B. *ḍāl*, Or. *ḍāḷa*; Mth. *ḍār* ' branch ', *°ri* ' twig '; Aw. lakh. *ḍār* ' branch ', H. *ḍāl*, *°lā* m., G.*ḍāḷ*, *°ḷī* f., *°ḷũ* n. 2. A. *ṭhāl* ' branch ', *°li* ' twig '; H. *ṭhāl*, *°lā* m. ' leafy branch (esp. one lopped off) '. 3. Bhoj. *ḍāṛhī* ' branch '; M. *ḍāhaḷ* m. ' loppings of trees ', *ḍāhḷā* m. ' leafy branch ', *°ḷī* f. ' twig ', *ḍhāḷā* m. ' sprig ', *°ḷī* f. ' branch '. *ḍāla -- 2 ' basket ' see *ḍalla -- 2.1. S.kcch. *ḍār* f. ' branch of a tree '; WPah.kṭg. *ḍāḷ* m. ' tree ', J. *ḍā l* m.; kṭg. *ḍaḷi* f. ' branch, stalk ', *ḍaḷṭi* f. ' shoot '; A. *ḍāl* (phonet. *d* --) ' branch ' (CDIAL 5546)

ढाळा [ḍhāḷā] *m* A small leafy branch, spring. 2 A plant of gram, sometimes of वाटाणा, or of लांक.

ढाळी [ḍhāḷī] *f* A branch or bough.P. *ḍhālaṇā* ' to pour, throw, melt '; Ku. *ḍhālṇo* ' to fill, throw, cut down '; N. *ḍhālnu* ' to fell '; A. *ḍhāliba* ' to pour ', B. *ḍhālā*,

Or. *ḍhāḷibā*, Mth. *ḍhārab*, Bhoj. *ḍhāral*, H.*ḍhārnā*, *ḍhālnā*, G. *ḍhāḷvũ*, M. *ḍhāḷṇẽ* ' to smooth the clods in a field, to shed its lustre (of a pearl) '. *ḍhalla -- ' lump ' see *ḍala -- .1. WPah.kṭg. *ḍhɔ̀ḷnõ* ' to fall, set (of sun), flow ', J. *ḍhaḷṇu*. 2. *ḍhālayati: WPah.kṭg. *ḍhàḷnõ* ' to throw, pour down, chop (wood) '; J. *ḍhāḷṇu* ' to cause to melt '.(CDIAL 5581).

ḍhāla n. ' shield ' lex. 2. *ḍhāllā -- . 1. Tir. (Leech) "*dàl*" ' shield ', Bshk. *ḍāl*, Ku. *ḍhāl*, gng. *ḍhāw*, N. A. B. *ḍhāl*, Or. *ḍhāḷa*, Mth. H. *ḍhāl* m.2. Sh. *ḍal* (pl. *°lẹ̄*) f., K. *ḍāl* f., S. *ḍhāla*, L. *ḍhāl* (pl. *°lā̃*) f., P. *ḍhāl* f., G. M. *ḍhāl* f. *ḍhāllā -- : WPah.kṭg. (kc.) *ḍhā`l* f. (obl. -- *a*) ' shield ' (a word used in salutation), J. *ḍhāl* f. (CDIAL 5583).

ढाल [ḍhāla] *f* (S through H) A shield. 2 The grand flag of an army directing its march and encampments: also the standard or banner of a chieftain: also a flag flying on forts &c. *v* दे. (Marathi) ढालकाठी [ḍhālakāṭhī] *f* ढालखांब *m* A flagstaff; esp.the pole for a grand flag or standard. 2 fig. The leading and sustaining member of a household or other commonwealth.

ढालपट्टा [ḍhālapaṭṭā] *m* (Shield and sword.) A soldier's accoutrements comprehensively. (Marathi)

करडूं or करडें [karaḍū or ṅkaraḍēṃ] *n* A kid. (Marathi)
करडा [karaḍā] *a* Hard from alloy--iron, silver &c. (Marathi) Apabhraṃśa (*Jasaharacariu*) karaḍa- hard.

Ta. karaṭu roughness, unevenness, churlish temper; karaṭṭu rugged, uneven, unpolished; karaṇ uneven surface in vegetables and fruits, scar;karu prong, barb, spike; karumai, karil severity, cruelty; karukku teeth of a saw or sickle, jagged edge of palmyra leaf-stalk, sharpness. *Ma.*karaṭu what is rough or uneven; kaṟu rough; kaṟuppu roughness; karuma sharpness of sword; karukku teeth of a saw or file, thorns of a palmyra branch, irregular surface; karukarukka to be harsh, sharp, rough, irritating; karikku edge of teeth; kari-muḷ hard thorn; projecting parts of the skin of custard-apples, jack-fruits, etc.; kari-maṭal rind of jack-fruits. *Ko.* karp keenness or harshness (of wind); ? kako·ṭ hoe with sharp, broad blade (for -ko·ṭ, see 2064). *Ka.* karaḍu that is rough, uneven, unpolished, hard, or waste, useless, or wicked; kaṟaku, karku, kakku, gaṟaku, garaku, garku, garasu a jag, notch, dent, toothed part of a file or saw, rough part of a millstone, irregular surface, sharpness. *Tu.* karaḍů, karaḍu rough, coarse, worn out; wastage, loss, wear; kargōṭa hardness, hard-heartedness; hard, hard-hearted; garu rough; garime severity, strictness; gargāsů a saw. *Te.* kara sharp; karagasamu a saw; karakasa roughness; karusu rough, harsh; harsh words; kaṟaku, kaṟuku harshness, roughness, sharpness; rough, harsh, sharp; gari hardness, stiffness, sharpness; (B.) karaṭi stubborn, brutish, villainous; kakku a notch or dent, toothed part of a saw, file, or sickle, roughness of a millstone. *Go.* (Ma.) karkara sharp (*Voc.* 543). *Kur.* karcnā to be tough, (Hahn) be hardened. ? Cf. 1260 Ka. garasu. / Cf. Skt. karaṭa- a low, unruly, diffioult poroon; karkara hord, firm; karkaśa- rough, harsh, hard; krakaca-, karapattra- saw; khara-hard, harsh, rough, sharp-edged; kharu- harsh, cruel; Pali kakaca- saw; khara- rough; saw; Pkt. karakaya- saw; Apabhraṃśa (*Jasaharacariu*) karaḍa- hard. Cf. esp. Turner, *CDIAL*, no. 2819. Cf. also Skt. karavāla- sword (for second element, cf. 5376 Ta. vāḷ).(DEDR 1265).

1266 *Ta.* karaṭu ankle, knot in wood. *Ma.* karaṇa knot of sugar-cane; kuraṭṭa knuckle of hand or foot. *Ka.* karaṇe, kaṇṇe clot, lump. *Te.* karuḍu lump, mass, clot.

ścandrá ' shining ' in *puru -- ścandrá --* , *su -- ścandrá --* , &c. RV. [√ścand1]
Paš. *čhandaläiki* ' lamp, torch (?) ' IIFL iii 3, 49.(CDIAl 12654).

<kol>,,<kul>\\<kolla>,,<kulla>(L) {N} ``^terrapin, ^tortoise, ^turtle''. !(not in Ram.). #40312.

várti1 (and *vartí --*) f. ' wick ' MBh., ' small compress ' Suśr., ' lamp ' lex., *°ikā --* f. ' wick ' KālP. [√vr̥t1]
Pa. *vaṭṭi --* , *°ikā --* f. ' wick ', Pk. *vaṭṭī --* , *°ṭiā --* , *vatti --* f.; Sh. *batī*´ ' unlit native lamp, candle, wick of

European lamp ' (← H.?); S. *vaṭi* f. ' wick '; L. *vaṭṭ* f. ' roll of grass, wick ', awāṇ. *vaṭ* ' wick ', P. *vaṭṭī*, *ba°*, *battī* f.; N. *bāti* ' lamp ' (*bati* ← H.), A. *bāti*, B. *bāti* ' wick, lamp, candle '; Or. *bati* ' lamp ' (← H.), Bi. Mth. Bhoj. *bātī*, OAw. *bātī* ' wick ', H. *bātī*, *battī* f. (→ N. Or. and prob. Sh.); G. *vāṭ* f. ' lamp ', *vātī* f. ' perfumed match or taper '; M. *vāt* f. ' wick ', Ko. *vāti*, Si. *väṭ -- a* ' lamp ', *väṭi -- ya* ' wick '; Md. *vo'* ' lamp '; -- with -- *o* as from an orig. masculine: Ku.*bāto* m. ' wick, lamp '; N. *bāto* ' rope of twisted cane (to tie down thatch) '. dīpavarti -- , *pādavarti -- , *saṁdhyāvartikā -- .S.kcch. *batī*, *bhatī* f. ' lamp, torch ' ← H.; WPah.kṭg. *batti*, kc. *baṭe* f. ' wick, lamp, light ', J. *bāṭī* f. (CDIAL 11359).

Kuwi (Su.) hūḍ- (-it-) to burn, shoot with gun; (F.) hūdali to burn; (S.) hūtinai to burn, kindle. *Kur.* kuṛnā (kuṭṭas) to grow warm, become hot, be heated; cook (*tr.*) on live embers, bake on an open fire. *Malt.* kuṛe (kuṭ-) to burn, roast, sear; kuṛnare to be hot or warm; kuṛni warm, hot.(DEDR 2654).

kuṭa1 m.n. ' water -- pot, pitcher ' Yaśast., *kūṭa* -- 5 n. lex., *kuḍikā* -- f. lex. 2. *kuṭava -- . 3. *kōṭa -- 4. [With kuṇḍá -- 1, *kulla --3, kúlāla -- , *kōḍamba -- , gōla -- 2, *ghōla -- 2 ← Drav. EWA i 221, 226 with lit. -- Cf. kuḍava --] 1. Pa. *kuṭa* -- m.n. ' pitcher '; NiDoc. *kuḍ'a* ' waterpot ', Pk. *kuḍa* -- m.; Paš. *kuṛā̃* ' clay pot ' (or < kuṇḍá -- 1); Kal. *kŕūṛi* ' milking pail '; H.*kuliyā* f. ' small earthen cup '; Si. *kuḷāva* ' pot, vessel for oil ' (EGS 47 wrongly < kaṭāha --), *kaḷa -- geḍiya* ' waterpot ', *kaḷaya* (or < kaláśa --).2. Pa. *kuṭava* -- ' nest ' (semant. cf. N. *gũṛ* s.v. kuṇḍá -- 1); Or. *kuṛuā* ' tall red earthen pot for cooking curry and rice offerings in the temple at Puri '.3. Pk. *kōḍaya* -- , *°ḍia* -- n. ' small earthen pot '; Dm. *kōŕí* ' milking pail '; G. *koṛiyũ* n. ' earthen cup for oil and wick '; M. *koḍẽ* n. ' earthen saucer for a lamp '.(CDIAL 3227).

OMarw. (Vīsaḷa) loc.sg.m. *kūṛaï* ' pot '; G. *kuṛlī* f. ' small pitcher '.kuṭa2, *°ṭi* -- , *°ṭha* -- 3, *°ṭhi* -- m. ' tree ' lex., *°ṭaka* -- m. ' a kind of tree ' Kauś.Pk. *kuḍa* -- m. ' tree '; Paš. lauṛ. *kuṛā´* ' tree ', dar. *kaṛék* ' tree, oak ' ~ Par. *kōṛ* ' stick ' IIFL iii 3, 98.(CDIAL 3228).

jyṓtis n. ' light, moonlight ' RV., ' heavenly body ' Mn. [~ *dyōtis* -- n. ' light, star ' lex. -- √jyut] Pa. *jōti* -- n.m. ' light, star, fire '; Aś. shah. *jotikaṁdhani* ' masses of light '; Pk. *jōi* -- m. ' light, fire ', *jōī̆-* f. ' lightning ', *jōisa* -- n. ' constellation '; A. *zūi* ' fire, lamp, spark, firefly '; B. *jũi* ' fire '; Or. *joe, joi, jui* ' fire, cremation fire, pit over which cremation pile is placed '; M. *ǰov* f. ' lightning '; Si. *dō* ' light, star '.WPah. sat. *ǰōˇth* ' moon '; kṭg. *ǰótth* f., Wkc. *ǰɔ̄th* f. in phrases ' moon is waxing, waning '; J. *joti* f. ' light of sun or lamp ' -- all ← Sk., partly X WPah.kṭg. *ǰɔṇ* ' moonlight ' < jyṓtsnā -- .(CDIAL 5300).

jyōtáyati ' illuminates ' AV. [~ *dyōtayati* MBh. - √jyut]Or. *joebā* ' to kindle a fire '; H. poet. *joyanā* ' to burn, set fire to '.(CDIAL 5296).

jvālá m. ' light, torch ' Kauś., ' flame ' MBh., *jvālā* -- f. KātyŚr. 2. *juvāla -- . [~ *jvāra -- . -- √jval] 1. Pa. *jāla* -- m. ' glow, blaze ', *°lā* f. ' flame '; Pk. *jāla* -- , *°laya* -- m. ' flame, fire ', *°lā* -- f. ' flame '; Paš. ar. *ǰiāel* ' flame '; K. *zāl* f. ' fever '; A.*zāl* ' heat of fire for cooking, heat, ray of light '; B. *jāl* ' flame of a fire '; Or. *jāḷā* ' burning sensation, inflammation '; M. *ǰāḷ* m. ' flame, fire, fever, passion '; Si. *dalaya, daluva, dalla* ' flame, effulgence '.2. Bshk. *ǰūl* ' iron lamp '; Ku. *jwālo* ' flame ', N. *juwālo, jwālo* (ND 226 b 26 wrongly ← Sk.). Ko. *ǰāḷa* n.pl. ' entry '; -- *ǰaḷāra* ' mosquito ' < **jvālākāra* -- ? (CDIAL 5312).

*jvālana ' kindling '. [√jval]K. *zālun* m. ' fuel '; Bhoj. *jāran* ' burning of spices '; H. *jāran* m. ' firewood '; M. *ǰāḷaṇ* n. ' fuel '.(CDIAL 5313).

jvālayati ' sets on fire ' MBh. [√jval]
Pa. *jālēti*, Pk. *jālēi*, Gaw. *zala* -- ' to light a fire '; K. *zālun* ' to set on fire '; P. *jāḷnā, jālaṇā* ' to kindle '; WPah. bhal. *ǰāṇū* tr. ' to burn '; A. *zāliba* ' to kindle ', B. *jālā*, Or. *jāḷibā*; Bi. *jārab* ' to burn, esp. cremate a corpse '; Mth. *jārab* tr. ' to burn ' (→ N. *jārnu* ' to burn to ashes '), OAw.*jārai*; H. *jālnā, jārnā*, OMarw. *jālai*; M. *ǰāḷṇẽ* ' to burn, annoy '.WPah.kṭg. (kc.) *ǰaḷnõ* tr. ' to burn, kindle, set on fire '. (CDIAL 5314).

jvālita ' set alight '. [√jval] Pa. *jālita* -- ; Si. *dälla*, st. *däli* -- ' flame '. (CDIAL 5315).

Ta. mātaḷai, mātuḷai, mātuḷam pomegranate. *Ma.* mātaḷam id. (DEDR 4809). dāḍima m. ' pomegranate tree ' MBh., n. ' its fruit ' Suśr., *dālima* -- m. Amar., *ḍālima* -- lex. 2. dāḍimba -- m. lex. 3. *dāṇḍu -- . 1. Pa. *dālima* -- m., NiDoc. *daḍ'ima*, Pk. *dāḍima* -- , *dālima* -- n., *dāḍimī* -- f. ' the tree ', Dm. *dā̤ṙim*, Shum. Gaw. *dā´ṛim*, Kal. *dā̤ṙəm*, Kho. *dáḷum*, Phal. *dhe_ṛum*, S. *ḍāṛhū̃* m., P. *dāṛū̃*, *°ṛū̃*, *°ṛam* m., kgr. *dariūṇ* (= *dariū̃*?) m.; WPah. bhiḍ. *de_ṛū̃* n. ' sour pomegranate '; (Joshi) *dāṛū̃*, OAw. *dārivaṁ* m., H. poet. *dāriū̃* m., OG.*dāḍimi* f. ' the tree ', G. *dāṛam* n., *dāṛem* f. ' the tree ', Si. *deḷum*.2. WPah.jaun. *dāṛim*, Ku. *dāṛim*, *dālim*, *dālimo*, N. *dārim*, A. *ḍālim*, B. *dāṛim*, *dālim*, Or. *dāḷimba*, *°ima*, *dāṛima*, *ḍāḷimba*, *ḍarami* ' tree and fruit '; Mth. *dāṛim* ' pomegranate ', *daṛimı* ' dried mango '; H. *dāṛimb*, *°im*, *dālim*, *ḍāṛim*, *ḍār°*, *ḍāl°* m.,

M. *dāḷīb*, *°ḷīm*, *ḍāḷīb* n. ' the fruit ', f. ' the tree '. 3. Sh.gil. *daṇū* m. ' pomegranate ', *daṇúi* f. +' the tree ', jij. *ḍ*lṇəi*, K. *dönü* m., P. *dānū* m. Garh. *dāḷimu* ' pomegranate ', A. *ḍālim* (phonet. *d* --).(CDIAL 6254).

*prabhāla ' light '. [Cf. *bhāla* -- 3 n. ' splendour ' Inscr. -- prabhā´ -- : √ bhā] Dm. *pral* ' light '; Gaw. *plal*, *plɔl* ' light, iris of eye ', adj. ' light, bright '; Kal. Leitner) *pralik*, rumb. *prelík* ' light ', Bshk. *čāl*, *čäl*, Chil. *čulo*; Sv.*plal* adj. ' light, bright '; Gau. *čou* sb., Phal. *prāl*; Sh. *ç̣alō* m. ' lighted torch ' (on ac. of *a* and *ō* perh. rather < *pralōka --); N. *pālā* ' lamp ' AO xviii 230. (CDIAL 8711)

``^bright":

So. *ta'ar*(R) `to shine, to be bright, to bloom'.

So. *tar*(R) `white'.

Gu. *tara:dutu* `light'.

Kh. *tardi* `to light a lamp, lamp light, a lamp'.

Mu. *TaTi* `a lamp'.

Bh. *ThaThi* `earthen lamp'.

@(C188)

<tar> {V} ``to ^whiten, to ^clean''. @W0381. {So.<ta'ar>. #23751.

<tara>,,<tara?>,, <taraD> {N} ``^light (^daylight, ^sunlight, ^lamp-light)''. {ADJ} ``^light, ^bright''. {V} ``to become id., to ^dawn''. Cf. <tar> `whiten', <taras> `twilight'. @N0438,N1017,W0382. ??forms-classes are ordered resp'ly. #23760.

<tara-bela> {N} ``^dawn''. |<bela> `time'. @:. #2423.

<par-bela tara-bela> {N} ``^dawn''. |<par-bela> `dawn?'. @N0439. #2434.

<muTla-tara> {N} ``(a certain?) ^constellation''. |<muTla> `club'. @N0462. #15742.

Kh<camkha>(AD) {NI} ``^lamp_^holder''.
Kh<camke>(ABD) {VI} ``to ^flash, to ^shine; to be ^flat''. Syn.<cikno>(A), <cikron>(D), <ci~kRo>(B).

<dipO>(MP) {N} ``^lamp''. *Kh.<diom>(A), ~<diyom>(B) `earthenware lamp', Mu.<dia>, H.<dIya>, ~<dipΛ>, O.<dipO>, Sk.<dipΛ>. %8861. #8781 <diom>(A),,<diyom>(B) {NI} ``earthenware

^lamp". *@. ??VAR. #8081. <diva> {N} ``small clay ^lamp". @5204. #7631.

dīpa m. ‘ lamp ’ ĀśvGr̥., *°paka* -- m., *°pikā* -- f. Hariv. [√dīp] Pa. *dīpa* -- , *°paka* -- m., *°pikā* -- f., Pk. *dīva* -- , *°vaya* -- m., *°vī* -- , *°viā* -- f., Ḍ. *dīa* m.; Ash. *diwā* ‘ torch (of pine wood) ’, Wg. *dēw*; S. *ḏio* m. ‘ lamp ’, L. *ḏivā* m. (→ Kho. *dīwa*, Sh.koh. *ḍevā*), khet. awāṇ. *dīvā* m., P. *dīvā*, *dīā* m., Ku. *diyo* m., gng. *dyū*, N. *diyo*, B. *diyā*, Or. dial. *ḍiā*; Bi.*dīyā* ‘ lamp -- saucer ’; Mth. *dīā* ‘ lamp ’, Aw.lakh. *diā*, H. *dīwā*, *dīyā* m.; G. *dīvɔ* m. ‘ lamp ’, *dīvī* f. ‘ lampstand ’; M. *divā* m. ‘ lamp ’, *divī* f., Si.*diva.* -- Ext. -- *ḍa* -- : K. *zuvürü* f. ‘ lampstand ’; Or. *diuṛā*, *°ṛi* ‘ torch, handlamp ’; Bi. *diurī*, *diyarī*, *dīrī* ‘ very small lamp -- saucer ’; G. *divṛɔ* m. ‘ lamp made of wheat -- flour ’; -- -- *l* -- : Bi. *diulī* ‘ small lamp -- saucer ’; H. *dīwlā* m., *°lī* f., *dewlā* m., *°lī* f. ‘ small lamp, socket ’.S.kcch. *ḍīyo* m. ‘ lamp ’, WPah.poet. *diu*, kṭg. *diwɔ*, *diɔ* m., J. *dīwā* m.; Garh. *diu* ‘ earthen lamp ’; OMarw. *diva* ‘ lamp ’. (CDIAL 6348) dīpana ‘ kindling ’ MBh. [√dīp]Cf. Aś.shah. man. *dipana*, gir. *dīpanā* f. ‘ glorification ’; -- Pk. *dīvaṇa* -- n., *°ṇā* -- f. ‘ lighting ’; K. *zyunu*, dat. *zinis* m. ‘ firewood ’; WPah.bhal.*dīuṇī* f. ‘ brazier on a stand on which pine wood is burnt to give light ’; H. *diyanā* m. ‘ lamp ’.(CDIAL 6352).

*dīparukṣa ‘ lampstand ’. [~ dīpavr̥kṣa -- . -- dīpa -- , *rukṣa --] Pa. *dīparukkha* -- m. ‘ lampstand ’, L.awāṇ. *drōkhā* m., poṭh. *darokhā* m., B. *derkhuyā*, *°kho* (ODBL 324 < **dīparakṣa* --); Or. (Sambhalpur)*dirkhā* ‘ niche in wall ’; Bi. *diarakh*, *dekhar*, *diarkhā*, *dẽkhrā* ‘ wall -- bracket for lamp ’, H. *deorkhā* m. (CDIAL 6353).

dīpavarti f. ‘ lamp -- wick ’ Daś. [dīpa -- , várti -- 1] S. *ḍiāṭī* f. ‘ torch, kind of lamp ’; L. *ḍīvaṭ*, *°ṭī* f. ‘ candlestick, light -- holder ’, awāṇ. *diuṭ*, *ḍīvuṭ* ‘ wick ’; P. *ḍīūṭ*, *dīuṭ*, *dīvaṭ* f. ‘ lampstand ’, WPah.cam. *dīūṭā*; B. *diuṭi*, *deu°* ‘ lamp, torch ’; B. *dīwaṭ*, *dīyaṭ* ‘ lamp -- stand ’, Bhoj. *ḍiyaṭi*, Aw.lakh. *ḍiaṭi* (EA 45 < **dīpapaṭṭikā* --), H.*dīwaṭ*, *dew°* f.; G. *diveṭ* f. ‘ wick ’; M. *divṭā* m., *°ṭī* f. ‘ torch made of oiled cloth round a stick '. -- Deriv.: B. *diuṭiyā* ' torch -- bearer ';

OG.*dīvaṭīu* m. ' servant carrying a torch before a king '

(CDIAL 6354)

<butti-toD>(L) {N} ``a ^lamp called a dibiri''.

*Or.<bOti>K. #19141.

<bambaRa> {N} ``^wick of a lamp or lantern''.

@6619. #2611.

ಅಕ್ಕಸಾಲೆ akka-sâlĕ. = ಅಕಸಾಲೆ, etc. The workshop of a goldsmith (T. ಅಕ್ಕಶಾಲೈ, a shop where metals are worked). 2, a goldsmith (ನಾಡಿಸ್ಥಮು, ಸ್ವರ್ಣಕಾರ, ಕಲಾದ, etc. Nr.; Hlâ.; Mr. 376; C.). ಪದಕಮನ್ ಅಕ್ಕಸಾಲೆಯಿಂ ಮಾಡೆ ಪಟ್ಟುದು (Śmd. 157). ಮಾಡಿದಂ ಪದಕಮನ್ ಅಕ್ಕಸಾಲೆ (301). ಕೊಳುವ ಕೊಡುವ ಎಡೆಯಲ್ಲಿ ಅರಿದಡೆ ಮೊಳೆಗಳಂ ಹೊಡಿ ನೋಂಕೆ, ಒಳ್ಳಿಹ ಮೊಳೆಯನ್ ಒರೆಗೊಪ್ಪು ಅಕ್ಕಸಾಲೆಯು (Bp. 21, 30). ಅಕ್ಕಸಾಲೆಗಿನ್ತ ಕಳ್ಳನಿಲ್ಲ, ಮುಕ್ಕಗದ್ದೆಗಿನ್ತ ಬೆಳೆಯಿಲ್ಲ (Prv.). — ಅಕ್ಕಸಾಲೆಯ. -ಅ 3. = ಅಕ್ಕಸಾಲ (My.; T. ಅಕ್ಕಶಾಲೈಯ). ಅಕ್ಕಸಾಲೆಯುರ ಸಲಾಕೆ (G. 62. 65). ಅಕ್ಕಸಾಲೆಯನ್ ಊರಿಗೊಕ್ಕಲ್ ಎಣ್ಣಿಸ ಬೇಡ! ಬೆಕ್ಕು ಬಸ್ಸಿಲಿಯ ಹಿಡಿವನ್ತೆ; ಊರಿಂಗೆ ರಕ್ಕಸನಹನು (Sp.). — ಅಕ್ಕಸಾಲೆಯವ. -ಅವ. = ಅಕ್ಕಸಾಲೆಯ. (My.; ಕಂಸಾಳಕ, ಕಂಸಾಳೆ, ಕಲಾದ, ನಾಡಿಸ್ಥಮು G.).

అగసాలి [agasāli] or అగసాలెవాడు *agasāli.* [Tel.] n. A

goldsmith. కంసాలివాడు. (Telugu)

उशनस् uśanas. *m.* [वश्-कनसि संप्र° Uṇ.4.238] (Nom. sing. उशना; Voc. sing. उशनन्, उशन, उशनः) N. of Śukra, regent of the planet Venus, son of Bhṛigu and precep- tor of the Asuras. In the Vedas he has the epithet (or patronymic name) *Kāvya* given to him, probably because he was noted for his wisdom; मित्रावरुणावुशनां काव्यम् (अवथः) Av.4.29.6. cf. कवीनामुशना कविः Bg. 1.37; He is also known as a writer on civil and reli- gious law (Y.1.4). and as an authority on civil polity; शास्त्रमुशनसा प्रणीतम् Pt.5; अध्यापितस्योशनसापि नीतिम् Ku.3.6. -Comp. -प्रियम् A kind of gem Called गोमेद (वैडूर्य ?)(Apte lexicon)

ūṣmán m. ' heat, steam ' AV., *uṣman* -- m., *ūṣmā* -- f. MBh., *°maka* -- m. lex. [√vas3]Pa. *usumā* -- , *usmā* -- f. ' heat ', Pk. *umha* -- m., *°hā* -- f., K. *wūhü*, *ṳ̄hü* f.; S. *usa* f. ' sunshine '; L. *huss* f., *hussaṛ* m. ' sultriness ', awāṇ. *hussuṛ* ' sultry ' (← WPah. bhal. *hussaṛ* f. ' heat '); EP. *hummh* m. ' sultriness '; A. *um* ' gentle heat '; G. *ūph* f. ' warmth ', *hūph* f. ' genial warmth '; Ko. *hūma* ' sweat '. – (CDIAL 2441). uṣṇá1 ' hot ' RV., *°aka* -- m. ' heat ' Pat. [√vas3]Pa. *uṇha* -- , Pk. *uṇha* -- , *usiṇa* -- ' hot ', m. ' heat '; K. *wuśunu*,

f. *°śüñü* ' warm, hot '; H. *unāh* m. ' hot vapour, steam '; G. *ūnũ, hunũ* ' hot, warm '; M. *ūnh, ūn* ' hot ', n. ' heat of sun ', redup. *ūnhūnh, unhan* ' burning hot '; Ko. *hūna* ' hot '; Si. *uṇu* ' hot ', *uṇa* ' fever '. -- P. ludh. *huṭṭ* ' sultry ' rather < uṣṭa -- 2. 1: Md. *hūnu* ' hot '.(CDIAL 2389). *uṣṇapānīya ' hot water '. [uṣṇá -- 1, pānī´ya --]M. *unhvaṇī* n. ' water heated in the sun's rays '.(CDIAL 2393). uṣṇayati ' heats ' MW. 2. *uṣṇāpana -- ' contraption for heating '. [uṣṇá -- 1] usrá m. ' ray, sun, day ', *usŕ* -- f. ' morning light ', *usrā´* -- f. ' daybreak, cow ' RV. [√vas3] Pk. *usa* -- m. ' ray ', *ussā* -- f. ' cow '; M. *ustẽ* n. ' first morning light ' (-- *tẽ* < tḗjas --).(CDIAL 2399). 1. MB. *unāe* ' gets hot '.2. B. *unān, unan, unun* ' oven, fireplace '; G. *unāmṇɔ* m., *°ṇiyũ* n. ' pot for heating bath water in '.(CDIAL 2394).

śúṣka ' dried ' RV., *śuṣkaka* -- R. [√śuṣ1]Pa. *sukkha* -- ' dry ', Pk. *sukkha* -- , *sukka* -- , *suṁkha* -- ; NiDoc. *śukha, śuka* ' epithet of wine '; Gy. eur. *šuko* ' dry, thin ', pal. _škă_ ' dry, hard ' (< *_ṣuṣka_ --); Dm. _šukī_ ' dry ' (f.? -- if m., < _śuṣkita_ --), Tir. _səka_; Woṭ. _šuk_ ' dry ', sb. ' hay '; Gaw. _šukhá_ ' dry ', Bshk. _šukh_, Sv. _šukho_, Phal. _šuko_, Sh.gil. _šūku̯_, koh. _šŭkhŭ_, pales. jij. _šuku_, K. _họ̆khu_, f. _h&obrevdotdot;chü_, S. _suko_ (_suka_, °_kī_ f. ' drought '), L. _sukkā_, khet. _sukhā_, P. _sukkā_ (_sukkaṛ_ ' lean, emaciated), WPah.jaun. _sūkhō_, Ku. _sukho_, _suko_, gng. _śukh_, N. _suko_, B. _sukhā_; Or. _suk_ ' dry, waterless ', _sukha_ ' waterless place ', _sukhā rukhā_ ' dry and rough '; Aw.lakh. _sūkh_ ' dry '; H. _sūkhā_,_sūkā_ ' dry ', m. ' dry land '; G. _sūkũ_ ' dry, lean '; M. _sukā_ ' dry ', _sukhā rukhā_ ' dry and rough '; Ko. _sukkẽ_ ' dry ', Si. _siku_, _hiku_, Md. _hiki_ (< *_śuṣkita_ -- ?); -- Pk._sukkhāṇa<-->_ ' dry ', A. _xukān_. -- Ext. -- _ll_ -- : Tor. _šugil_ ' dry '; Or. _sukhilā_ ' dried, withered '; -- -- _ṭṭ_ -- : N. _sukuṭe_ ' emaciated '; B. _sukṭiyā_ ' dried up ', Or. H._sukṭā_, M. _sukaṭ_; N. _sukuṭi_ ' dried meat or fish '; A. _xukaṭi_ ' dried fish ', B. _sukṭi_, _sũṭki_, Or. Mth. H. M. _sukṭī_ f. WPah.ktg. _śúkkhɔ_, kc. _śūkho_ ' dry ', A. _śukān_ (phonet. _x_ --). (CDIAL

12548) śuṣi1 f. ' drying ' lex. [√śuṣ1] Paš.kuṛ. *šeš* ' summer '?(CDIAL 12546). 12556 śuṣṇa ' *dry and hot ', m. ' demon (of drought?) ' RV., ' sun, fire ' lex. [~*śuṣṭa -- . -- √śuṣ1](CDIAL 12556). *śuṣṇakāra ' making hot '. [śuṣṇa -- , kāra -- 1]Dm. *šuṅgār* ' summer ' NTS xii 130.(CDIAL 12557). Ushyate 'to burn' (Sanskrit) *anús* ' day, daytime '(Khotanese); áhar n. ' day ', nom. *°ar*, loc. *áhan -- i* RV., pl. *áhas -- su* ŚBr. Pa. *aha* -- n., acc. *ahaṁ* and *ahō*; Pk. *aha* -- n., *ahō* ' by day ' (CDIAL 993).

śūka m.n. ' awn of grain ' R., ' bristle, spike (esp. of insects) ' W. [Cf. śuṅgā´ --] Pa. *sūka* -- m. ' awn of barley &c. '; Pk. *sūa* -- m. ' awn of rice &c. '; Wg. *šü* ' reed '; S. *suo* m. ' porcupine's quill '; L. *sūā* m. ' spit used in fishing '; P. *sūā* m. ' sprout, blade of grass, turner's spindle '; B. *sũā* ' tendril '; Or. *suā* ' beard of some grains, tendril ', *suā -- bāḷiā* ' hairy caterpillar '; H. *sūā*, *suwā* m. ' awn of grain, bristle, hair '. -- Ext. -- *l* -- : Pk. *sūala* -- n. ' awn of rice &c. '(CDIAL 12560).

śuṅgā´ f. ' sheath or calyx of young bud ' GṛS., ' awn of barley &c. ' lex. [Cf. śūka --]K. *hŏnga* f. ' root of a certain wild creeper (used medicinally for relief of fistula, ulcers and similar diseases) '; A. *xuṅ* ' awn of corn, anything pointed, clue '; B. *suṅg* ' awn, hair of caterpillar '; Or. *suṅga, suṅka* (X *śūka* -- ?) ' awn of barley &c. ', *suṅgā* ' hair of caterpillar '; Bi. *sũg, sũgh* ' beard of wheat '; -- ext. -- / -- : Kho. (Lor.) *šuṅgulu* ' ear of corn with grain in it ' (cf. Pk. *sūala* -- s.v. śūka --). -- Bi. (SMunger) *ṭũgnā* ' ear of wheat ', (North of Ganges) *ṭũgnī* ' cutting ears without stalks ' with variation of *ś* ~ *ṭ* discussed by W. Wüst RM 3, 8 ff. or poss. < *ṭuṇga -- 2.(CDIAL 12509).

śāṅkhika ' relating to a shell ' W. 2. *śāṅkhinī -- (*śaṅkhinī* -- f. ' mother -- of -- pearl ' Bālar.). [śaṅkhá -- 1]1. K. *hāngi* ' snail '; B. *sā̃khī* ' possessing or made of shells '.2. K. *hõgiñ* f. ' pearl oyster shell, shell of any aquatic mollusc '. (CDIAL 12380) śaṅkú1 m. ' peg, spike ' RV., ' stake, post ' MBh., ' stick, arrow ' Hariv.Pa. *saṅku* -- , *°uka* -- m. ' stake, spike, javelin ', Pk. *saṁku* -- m.; Dm. *šaṅ* ' branch, twig ', *šā̃kolī´* ' small do. ', Gaw. *šāṅkolī´*; Kal.rumb. *šoṅ* (st. *šoṅg* --), urt.*šaṅ* ' branch '; Kho. *šoṅg* ' a kind of shrub with white twigs (?) '; Phal. *šō̃ṅ* ' branch '; P. *saṅglā* m. ' a plank bridge in the hills '; A. *xā̃kāli* ' a kind of fishing spear '; Si. *aku -- va* ' stake '. -- X śā´khā -- : Gaw. *šā̃khá*, *šā̃ká* ' branch ', Sv. *šā̃khe*; OG. *sāṁkha* m. ' beam '. -- Connexion of the following is doubtful: S. *sā̃ga* f. ' one fork of a forked stick ', *sā̃gi* f. ' spear '; L. *sāṅg*, pl. *°gā̃* f. ' spear ', *sā̃golā* m. ' spear carried by a watchman '; P. *sā̃g* f. ' prong, fork, point ', *sāṅgī* f. ' pitchfork '; H.*sā̃g* f. ' spear, instrument for digging wells ', *sā̃gī* f. ' small spear '; G. M. *sā̃g* f. ' iron spear '.śaṅku -- 2 ' a partic. tree ' see śāka -- 1.Addenda: śaṅkú -- [Shgh. *x̌il ūng* ' stick ' not ← IA. e.g. Kho. *šoṅg* EVSh 102 where ref. to CDIAL is given wrongly as 12262](CDIAL 12260).

śaṅkhá1 m. (n. lex.) ' conch -- shell ' AV., *śaṅkhaka-* m.n. MBh.Pa. *saṅkha* -- m. ' conch, mother -- of -- pearl '; Pk. *saṁkha* -- m.n. ' conch ', *°khiyā* -- f. ' small do. '; S. *saṅghī* f. ' a kind of bracelet '; B. *sā̃kh* ' conch -- shell ',*sā̃khā, °kā, sẽkhā* ' conch bracelet ', Or. *saṅkhā*; OAw. *sāṁkha* m. ' conch -- shell ', H. *saṅkh* m., Si. *sak -- a, ha°.* -- Lws. in S. *saṅkhu* m. ' conch ', Ku. *sā̃kh,sā̃k.*Addenda: śaṅkhá -- 1 [*a* < non -- apophonic IE. *o* (Gk. ko/gxo*s*) T. Burrow BSOAS xxxviii 69] WPah.kṭg. *śáṅkkh* m. ' conch ' ← H.; Md. *sangu* ← Ind.; A. *śā̃k* (phonet. *x* --) ' bracelet made of shells ' AFD 187. (CDIAL 12263).

śaṅkhakāra -- , *°aka* -- m. ' shell -- worker ' lex. [śaṅkhá -- 1, kāra -- 1] B. *sā̃k(h)āri* ' maker of conch -- shell bracelets '; Or. *saṅkhāri* ' shell -- worker '; -- or <śaṅkhadāraka -- m. ' shell -- cutter ' lex. [śaṅkhá -- 1, dāra -- 1](CDIAL 12265).

A

B

C

D

E

T

U

V

W

Z

[1] http://etcsl.orinst.ox.ac.uk/cgi-bin/etcsl.cgi?text=c.1.6.2&display=Crit&charenc=&lineid=c162.122#c162.122

[2] http://en.wikipedia.org/wiki/Ninib

[3] **See ETCSL:** ma2-gi4-lum=type of boat. http://etcsl.orinst.ox.ac.uk/cgi-bin/etcsl.cgi?searchword=l=ma2-gi4-lum%20p=N%20a=type@of@boat&charenc=gcirc&sortorder=textno&header=brief

[4] http://etcsl.orinst.ox.ac.uk/cgi-bin/etcsl.cgi?text=t.1.6.1#

[5] http://www.louvre.fr/en/routes/great-goddess

[6] https://dascolihum.com/uploads/Ancient_Near_East1020.ppt

[7] http://www.sfgate.com/news/article/Seed-of-extinct-date-palm-sprouts-after-2-000-2628668.php#page-1

[8] *Archaeology*, Vol. 12, 09012013, Daily News.

[9] http://popular-archaeology.com/issue/09012013/article/ancient-date-palm-tree-flourishes-again http://mbtimetraveler.com/2013/02/14/extinct-date-palm-sprouts-after-2000-years/

[10] Eliade, Mircea, 2004, *Shamanism: archaic techniques of ecstasy*, Princeton University Press, Princeton, 2004; 1991, Images and symbols: studies in religious symbolism (trans. Philip Mairet), Princeton University Press, Princeton, 1991; 1961, *The sacred and the profane: the nature of religion* (trans. Willard R. Trask), Harper Torchbooks, New York, 1961.

[11] Curtis, JE, H. McCall, D. Collon and L. al-Gailani Werr, 2002, *New light on Nimrud, Proceedings of the Nimrud Conference, 11-13 March 2002*, London, British Institute for the study of Iraq in association with the British Museum, After Fig. 13-a, p.103.

[12] After fig. 10 in Hussein, Muzahem M. and Amer Suleiman, 1999, Nimrud: a city of golden treasures, Baghdad, Directorate of antiquities and heritage)(cf. Gansell, Amy Rebecca, 2008, Women of ivory as embodiments of ancient Near Eastern ideals of feminine beauty during the early first millennium BCE, PhD disservation, History of Art and Architecture, Harvard University.

[13] http://www.metmuseum.org/collections/search-the-collections/324328

[14] Rehm 1997, p. 415, fig. 271, no. S11.

[15] Parpola, Simo, 1993, The Assyrian Tree of Life: Tracing the Origins of Jewish Monotheism and Greek Philosophy, Journal of Near Eastern Studies, Vol. 52, No. 3 (Jul., 1993), pp. 161-208. http://www.atour.com/education/pdf/SimoParpola-TheAssyrianTreeOfLife.pdf)

[16] Cooper, Jerrold S., Assyrian prophecies, the Assyrian tree, and the Mesopotamian Origin of Jewish Monotheism, Christian Theology, Gnosticism and Much More, 2000, JAOS, 120, no.3,

pp. 430-444). See:
http://enenuru.proboards.com/index.cgi?board=explore&action=display&thread=173

[17] Vgl. H. York, Heiligen Baum, D.O. Edzard (ed.), Reallexikon der Assyrologie und Vorderasiatischen Archaologie, Bd.4, Berlin 1975, 269-282.

[18] Kepinski, Christine, 1982, L'Arbre stylize en asie occidentale au 2e millenaire avant J.-C (Bibliotheque de la delegation archeologique francaise en Iraq, vol. 3, ISBN: 9782865380213. Editions Recherche sur les civilisatios, CulturesFrance, Paris, Nos. 891-94; 924-36.

[19] http://www.bible-history.com/ibh/images/thumbs/hazor-tree-of-life-date-palm-750-bc.jpg

[20] http://www.bible-history.com/ibh/images/thumbs/standard-from-hazor-snakes.jpg

[21] http://www.matrifocus.com/IMB04/spotlight.htm

[22]
http://www.religion.ucsb.edu/faculty/thomas/classes/rgst116c/taylor.pdf
http://www.city-data.com/forum/religion-spirituality/908093-were-adam-eve-created-mortal-immortal-4.html#ixzz2jeuzsoGQ

[23] Hestrin, Ruth, 1991, Understanding Ashera: exploring semitic iconography, BAS Library http://members.bib-arch.org/publication.asp?PubID=BSBA&Volume=17&Issue=05&ArticleID=04

[24] http://www.natgeocreative.com/photography/10 Cult stand from Taanach (Tell Ti'innik). 02469

[25] http://mv.vatican.va/3_EN/pages/x-Schede/MEZs/MEZs_Sala09_01_037.html

[26] http://www.haaretz.com/print-edition/news/3-000-year-old-altar-uncovered-at-philistine-site-suggests-cultural-links-to-jews-1.375305

[27] http://en.wikipedia.org/wiki/Tablet_of_Shamash#cite_note-Zawadzki2006-3

[28] http://en.wikipedia.org/wiki/Tablet_of_Shamash

[29] http://www.gutenberg.org/files/28876/28876-h/files/17323/17323-h/v3b.htm Maspero, G., 1893, History of Egypt, Chaldea, Syria, Babylonia and Assyria, Volume III (Part B), London, The Grolier Society.

[30] http://www.specialtyinterests.net/seal_impressions_ostracon.html

[31] http://www.specialtyinterests.net/seal_impressions_ostracon.html

[32] http://www.maravot.com/Phrygian1b.html

[33] Parpola, Simo, 1993, p.167.

[34] J.E. Reade, *Assyrian sculpture,* London, The British Museum Press, 1983. http://www.britishmuseum.org/explore/highlights/highlight_image.aspx?image=throne_relief.jpg&retpage=26628

[35] http://rbedrosian.com/embod_tools.htm Emboden Jr., William A., Ethnobotanical tools in the ancient Near East, An expanded

version of this paper was subsequently published in *Ethnobotany, Evolution of a Discipline* (Portland, Oregon, 1995), pp. 93-107 under the title "Art and Artifact as Ethnobotanical Tools in the Ancient Near East with Emphasis on Psychoactive Plants."

[36] http://www.metmuseum.org/collections/search-the-collections/329229

[37] http://historicconnections.webs.com/archaeologythebible.htm

[38] After Pottier, M.H., 1984, *Materiel funeraire e la Bactriane meridionale de l'Age du Bronze*, Paris, Editions Recherche sur les Civilisations: plate 20.150

[39] After Marie-Helene Pottier, 1984, *Materiel funeraire de la Bactriane meridionale de l'age du bronze*, Recherche sur les Civilizations, Memoire 36, Paris, fig. 21; Sarianidi, V.I., 1986, Le complexe culturel de Togolok 21 en Margiane, *Arts Asiatiques 41*: fig. 6,21; Potts, 1994, fig. 53,8; Amiet, 1986, fig. 132.

[40] D.T. Potts, South and Central Asian elements at Tell Abraq (Emirate of Umm al-Qaiwain, United Arab Emirates), c. 2200 BC—AD 400, in Asko Parpola and Petteri Koskikallio, *South Asian Archaeology 1993*: , pp. 615-666.

[41] After Fig. 7 Holly Pittman, 1984, *Art of the Bronze Age: Southeastern Iran, Western Central Asia, and the Indus Valley*, New York, The Metropolitan Museum of Art, pp. 29-30.

[42] Mitchell, TC, 1986, Indus and Gulf type seals from Ur in: Shaikha Haya Ali Al Khalifa and Michael Rice, 1986, Bahrain

through the ages: the archaeology, London, 280-1, no. 8 and fig. 112). Gadd, CJ, Seals of Ancient Indian style found at Ur, in: Possehl, GL, ed 1979, *Ancient Cities of the Indus*, Delhi, Vikas Publishing House, p. 117.

[43] Å. Sjöberg & E. Bergmann, The Collection of the Sumerian Temple Hymns (Locust Valley, 1969), p. 46.) http://www.maverickscience.com/arch-history.pdf

[44] http://www.louvrebible.org.uk/index.php/louvrebible/default/visiteguidee/libation-au-dieu-shamash-rubrique-menu-137

[45] http://www.cmaa-museum.org/meso13.html

[46] A person with a vase with overflowing water; sun sign. C. 18th cent. BCE. E. Porada,1971, Remarks on seals found in the Gulf states, Artibus Asiae, 33, 31-7.

[47] After Possehl, GL, 1986, Kulli: an exploration of an ancient civilization in South Asia, Centers of Civilization, I, Durham, NC: 46, fig. 18 (Mehi II.4.5), based on Stein 1931: pl. 30

[48] http://www.metmuseum.org/toah/ho/02/wam/hod_41.160.192.htm

[49] Bloomsfield's ed.n, xliv. cf. Bloomsfield, American Journal of Philology, 11, 355; 12,416; Roth, Festgruss an Bohtlingk, 98.

[50] See *Vedic Index*, I, p. 177.

[51] Fleet, JRAS, 63, 1894 proceedings, 86, plate, IA 25. 262; cf. Sohgaura copper plate/B.M. Barua. The Indian Historical Quarterly, ed. Narendra Nath Law. Reprint. 41.

[52] Hussein and Suleiman 1999, figs. 159-60.

[53] D. Collon, *First impressions: cylinder se* (London, The British Museum Press, 1987) http://www.britishmuseum.org/explore/highlights/highlight_image.aspx?image=ps028618.jpg&retpage=18910

[54] http://www.bisi.ac.uk/sites/bisi.localhost/files/Curtis_et_al_New_Light_On_Nimrud.pdf

[55] Elena Marinova & Simone Riehl, 2009, Carthamus species in the ancient Near East and south-eastern Europe: archaeobotanical evidence for their distribution and use as a source of oil, in: Vegel Hist Arcchaeobot (2009) 18: 341-349.

[56] Potts, DT, 1997, Mesopotamian civilization: the material foundations, Athlone Press, London, pp.65-66; loc. cit. Meissner 1891: 292-6.

[57] http://en.wikipedia.org/wiki/Pine_cone

[58] http://www.cmaa-museum.org/meso08.html

[59] http://www.cmaa-museum.org/meso06.html

[60] André-Salvini B., "Art of the first cities : The Third millenium B.C. from the Mediterranean to the Indus", Exposition, New York, The Metropolitan Museum of Art, 8 mai-17 août 2003, p. 440, n 313.

Barrelet M., "Taureaux et symbolique solaire", in Revue

d'Assyriologie et d'Archéologie orientale, 48, Paris, Presses Universitaires de France, 1954, pp. 16-27.
Caubet A., "Exposition des quatre grandes civilisations mondiales : La Mésopotamie entre le Tigre et l'Euphrate", Exposition itinérante, Setagaya, Musée d'art de Setagaya, 5 août 2000-3 décembre 2000, Fukuoka, Musée d'art asiatique de Fukuokua, 16 décembre 2000- 4 mars 2001, Tokyo : NKH, 2000, n 120.
Heuzey L., "Le taureau chaldéen androcéphale et la sculpture à incrustations", Monuments Piot, VII, 1900-1901, pp. 7-11 et planche I.
Parrot A., Tello, vingt campagnes de fouilles (1877- 1933), Paris, Albin Michel, 1948, p. 146, fig. 12b.
Huot J.-L., "The Man-Faced Bull L. 76. 17 of Larsa", in Sumer, 34, Bagdad, State Organization of Antiquities and Heritage, 1978, pp. 106- 108, fig. a.
Spycket A., La statuaire du Proche-Orient ancien, Leyde, Brill, 1981, p. 220, n 184, pl. 147. http://www.louvre.fr/en/oeuvre-notices/recumbent-bull-mans-head

[61] http://www.livius.org/la-ld/lamassu/lamassu.html

[62] http://www.historywiz.com/galleries/sumerianbull-lyre.html

[63] http://archaeology.about.com/od/mesopotamiaarchaeology/ss/royal_cemetery_at_ur_3.htm

[64] http://www.themorgan.org/collections/collections.asp?id=624

[65] http://www.flickr.com/photos/antiquitiesproject/4877925228/in/gallery-bhcmbailey-72157624936775089/

[66] http://members.westnet.com.au/gary-david-thompson/page9n.html

[67] http://highered.mcgraw-hill.com/sites/dl/free/0072556323/87443/mat5ch01p001_029.pdf

[68] http://classconnection.s3.amazonaws.com/474/flashcards/1953474/png/capture_d___e__cran_2012-10-02_a___1549301349219895162.png

[69] Zainab Bahrani, 2011, The graven image: representation in Babylonia and Assyria, University of Pennsylvania Press, p.192.

[70] http://www.engr.mun.ca/~asharan/bihar/ironage/ironageindia2.htm

[71] Tewari, Rakesh, 2003, Origins of iron working in India: new evidence from the central Ganga plan and eastern Vindhyas, pp. 536-545. http://www.antiquity.ac.uk/ProjGall/tewari/tewari.pdf

[72] Waw Allap, ISBN: AS-33

http://www.gorgiaspress.com/bookshop/pc-339-35-apkalu-angel.aspx

http://www.ashmol.ox.ac.uk/ash/amocats/anet/pdf-files/ANET-26Bronze1MesV.pdf

[73] After Jeremias 1929: 353, fig. 183; cf. Asko Parpola, 1984, *Deciphering the Indus Script*, Cambridge Univ. Press, Fig. 10.19, p. 190). http://www.gatewaystobabylon.com/essays/essayenkiworld.html

[74] http://enenuru.proboards.com/index.cgi?board=expel&action=display&thread=361

[75] http://www.britishmuseum.org/research/collection_online/collection_object_details/collection_image_gallery.aspx?partid=1&assetid=502223&objectid=369354

[76] Kalyanaraman, S., 2013, *Meluhha: A visible language*, Herndon, Sarasvati Research Center. http://tinyurl.com/mydusbr

[77] http://www.tcd.ie/nmes/assets/img/rotator/thirteen.jpg

[78] http://www.heritageinstitute.com/zoroastrianism/hormozgan/index.htm

[79] Potts, DT, 2004, Hormuz, *Encyclopaedia Iranica*. http://www.iranicaonline.org/articles/hormuz-i

[80] Potts, DT, 2012, *A companion to the archaeology of the ancient Near East*, Vol. I, Blackwell, pp. 184-185.

[81] Moorey, Peter Rooer Stuart, 1999, Ancient Mesopotamian Materials and Industries: the archaeological evidence, Eisenbrauns, p.316.

[82] http://www.learningsites.com/NWPalace/NWP_ABS-archit.htm

http://www.learningsites.com/NWPalace/NWP_ThRm_renders.html

www.ingramcontent.com/pod-product-compliance
Lightning Source LLC
Chambersburg PA
CBHW060454280326
41933CB00014B/2751